Mixed Media

Barrie Day

OXFORD

OXFORD
UNIVERSITY PRESS

Great Clarendon Street, Oxford OX2 6DP

Oxford University Press is a department of the University of Oxford.
It furthers the University's objective of excellence in research, scholarship,
and education by publishing worldwide in

Oxford New York

Athens Auckland Bangkok Bogotá Buenos Aires Calcutta
Cape Town Chennai Dar es Salaam Delhi Florence Hong Kong Istanbul
Karachi Kuala Lumpur Madrid Melbourne Mexico City Mumbai
Nairobi Paris São Paulo Shanghai Singapore Taipei Tokyo Toronto Warsaw

with associated companies in Berlin Ibadan

Oxford is a registered trade mark of Oxford University Press
in the UK and in certain other countries

ISBN 0 19 831455 8

Printed in Spain by Graficas Estella SA

Author's acknowledgements
Special thanks to my wife Sue for her unstinting support,
and to friends Jean Wirth, Wendi Hyde and Jeff Adams
for their advice on preliminary ideas.

Contents

1 Getting started   **6**

Different forms of media text   7

Decoding media texts   8

     Signs in media texts   8

     The four basic media codes   9

Looking at the type of text   10

Looking at audience   12

Looking at purpose   14

Looking at effectiveness   16

2 The code of still graphic images   **18**

The knowledge you already have   18

Learning zone   20

     Composition: putting messages in pictures   20

     Figure signs   22

     Shape and proportion   25

     Colour, texture, and lighting   26

     Viewpoint   28

     The impact of news photographs   31

     Two-step reading   32

Task zone   36

     Deconstruction tasks   36

     Construction tasks   38

3 The code of written language   **39**

The knowledge you already have   39

Learning zone   40

     Alliteration   40

     Assonance   40

     Adjective tag   41

Rhyme   41

Emotive language   42

Puns   43

Syntax and rhythm   44

Slang or chatty language   46

Imagery   46

Active and passive voice   47

Imperative verbs   48

Interrogative verbs   48

Representation and bias   49

Looking at newspapers   50

Task zone   56

Deconstruction task 1   56

Construction task 1   57

Deconstruction task 2   58

Construction task 2   59

4 **Written language and still graphic images**   61

The knowledge you already have   61

Task zone   62

The graphic novel   62

The magazine holiday advert   64

The leaflet   66

The internet website   68

Newspaper extracts   70

5 **The code of sound**   73

The knowledge you already have   73

Learning zone   74

What makes up the code of sound?   74

Speaking voices   75

Sound effects   82

Silence	84
Music	84
Radio advertising	88
Task zone	90
Deconstruction task	90
Construction task	92
6 The code of moving images	**93**
The knowledge you already have	93
Genre films	93
Learning zone	95
Constructing a film: telling a story in pictures and sound	95
The screenplay	95
Mise-en-scène	98
Lighting	104
Camera shots	106
Editing	108
The soundtrack	109
Task zone	111
Deconstruction case study 1: *A Close Shave*	111
Deconstruction case study 2: *Macbeth*	118
Construction task: film adaptation	125
Glossary	127
Acknowledgements	128

 Where you see this icon on a page, it means there is a photocopiable sheet that your teacher can give you to help with the activity.

Getting started

You're about to start some detective work.

You're about to crack some codes.

We're going to take a close look at the **media** and the codes used in making media messages.

The word 'media' is the plural of 'medium': a means of communication. In this book, the word 'media' especially refers to those means which are used to communicate with a mass of people. These are also called **mass media**. What sorts of media can you name?

Media play a huge part in our lives. They provide entertainment (through TV programmes, radio and films), and information (through TV, newspapers, and the internet). But they can also attempt to influence and persuade us – to buy a particular product, to vote for a political party, or to feel a certain way about a current issue.

We use the term **media text** to refer to any message sent by the media. A media text might be as long as a feature film or as short as a five-second radio jingle.

All media texts try to influence us: newspaper articles and advertisements are obvious examples which do this. But even when we watch a film, we are influenced by what we see – to feel excitement, fear, happiness, and a whole range of other emotions.

Because of this ability to influence us, media texts are hugely powerful. Decoding them – working out how they exert that power – can be a lot of fun. But it's also useful to know how media texts work, so that we can decide for ourselves how much power we are going to let them have over us.

This book attempts to show you how.

Different forms of media text

You experience media texts in a variety of ways. You might see them on a screen, hear them on a radio or see them in a magazine.

▽

1 With a partner, note down all the different media texts you took an interest in during the past week. For each one, write down what type of text it was, and the title – for instance:

Type of text	Title
TV news programme	Six O'Clock News
Computer game	
Music CD	

See how many different forms of media text you can list.

2 Now, with your list to help you, make your own version of the chart below, ticking the boxes to show how much time you spend using each medium you have on your list. This will start you thinking about how much you use the mass media in a typical week.

Media	Not much time	Quite a lot of time	A lot of time
Newspapers		✓	
Brochures	✓		
Posters			✓
Television			✓
Internet		✓	
Radio	✓		

3 Now pick out the mass medium which you use more than any other during a week. Can you explain why you use this medium so much?

Decoding media texts

You've looked at the different kinds of media texts there are around us. Now you can start looking at the messages contained in these texts and how they are put together. You'll find you already know a lot about media texts – but you may not have thought about how and why media texts are constructed.

Signs in media texts

Media texts are made up of **signs** which stand for different things, and which can be combined to have a particular effect on the reader. (Even if a media text is made up entirely of pictures, we say you **read** it.)

You will already be familiar with some signs: for example, look at this extract from a media text:

The writer of this text is trying to excite the reader – and one of the first clues to this is how many exclamation marks there are in the text. You probably picked up on the use of this sign without really noticing.

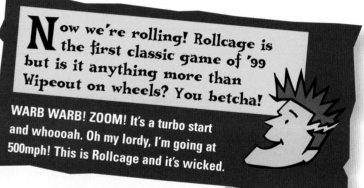

Now we're rolling! Rollcage is the first classic game of '99 but is it anything more than Wipeout on wheels? You betcha!

WARB WARB! ZOOM! It's a turbo start and whoooah. Oh my lordy, I'm going at 500mph! This is Rollcage and it's wicked.

Some signs in media texts can be quite difficult to spot and they can work in ways that it is hard to explain. However, let's start with some more signs which are all around us and which we can read very easily.

For instance, all of the following signs mean 'stop':

The full stop tells you when to stop reading.

Red traffic light   Stop sign   Traffic police hand sign   Full stop at end of sentence

Try to answer the following questions.

1 Which flowers are used as a sign of:
  a love?
  b remembering those killed in war?

2 Which colours are used as signs for:
  a death?
  b ambulance emergency warning?
  c traffic to 'go'?

3 Draw the graphic signs used in comics to indicate a character is:
  a thinking
  b speaking

4 Describe the audio (sound) signs which are used to represent the following:
  a danger (give three examples)
  b the breaking of a rule in a football game
  c telephone line engaged

5 Write down the meaning of the following signs. Have you read them in the same way as your partner?

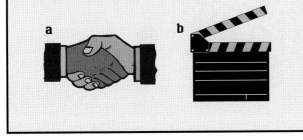

The signs we have just looked at are quite straightforward to read, because they are very familiar. The rest of this book will teach you about other signs which are used in media texts, and the ways they might work on the reader.

The four basic media codes

The signs used in media texts fall into four basic codes. Three of them are visual (we see the signs) and one is aural (we hear them). A media text will use one or more of these codes to get its message across.

Code of sound
Music, speech, sound effects, silence

Code of written language
Words, language features, punctuation

Code of moving images
Film, animation, TV, video and computer screen images

Code of still graphic images
Images drawn, photographed, computer generated

In the rest of this book we'll be looking at the signs that make up these four different codes, and how they combine to make media texts.

But you can start decoding media texts by asking some simple questions.

We'll look at these questions over the next few pages.

Looking at the type of text

The first questions you need to ask yourself about any media text are:

1 What type of text is this? (It might be a news report, a review, an advert, etc.)

2 What codes does this text use?

JFK'S SON KILLED IN PLANE CRASH

The son of murdered US President John F Kennedy is missing presumed dead in a plane crash.

Novice pilot John Kennedy Jr was flying his private aircraft when it plunged into the Atlantic.

1 Draw a five-column grid like the one shown below, and put the numbers of the texts on these two pages in the first column.

Look at the texts and answer the two questions above. Mark the second column 'type' and put your answer in it. You will fill in the rest of the grid as you work through the questions on the next few pages.

BBC Radio 1
FM 97.6-99.8
The Breakfast Show

Text	Type			
1				
2				
3				
3				
4				
5				
6				

Cinema film

④

The south will have a fair amount of cloud, but the sun will break through. In south Wales there will be outbreaks of light rain. Northern England and north Wales will have sunny spells.

⑤

⑥

With a superstar cast and break-through visual effects Dreamworks' spectacular comedy adventure, Antz, became 'king of the hill' with audiences and movie critics alike. Everyone digs Antz! Life is not a picnic for Z, a small worker ant with some very big ideas whose chances of landing the beautiful Princess Bala are literally one in a billion.

Looking at audience

The next question to ask yourself is:

Who was the media text produced for – who is its audience?

The audience for a media text can be classified using these questions:

1 Are they male or female – or does the text aim to attract either sex?

2 How old are they?

3 What sort of job do they do? Do they are earn a high, medium or low wage?

4 What are their interests? (e.g. Do they have families? Do they travel a lot, or have particular hobbies?)

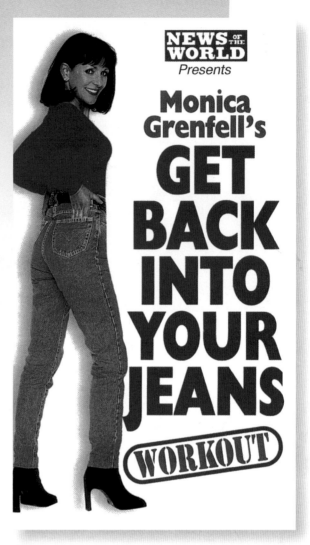

1 *Video*

Indiana Jones and the Infernal Machine

Lara with a hat and a whip? Hang on! Indy got there first when he raided a certain lost ark. Now he's followed Crofty to the PlayStation and his game's looking brill! It's 1947 and you have to stop the Russians and their sinisterly-named Infernal Machine. Indy gets to use not only his famous whip but huge bazookas in this great-looking 3D adventure!

2

✿ THE HOTTEST RESORT IN SPAIN! The 'WHITE COAST' of Benidorm boasts one of Europe's **FINEST** sunshine records and remains the **WILDEST** of all Costa Blanca's resorts. The panoramic sandy beaches of LEVANTE and PONIENTE have an excellent choice of water sports.☺

3

4 *Graphic novel*

1 Take a look at the texts on these two pages. Each one has been produced with a particular audience in mind.

For each of them, say who you think is the audience for the text. Then give reasons for your decision.

2 Now look back at the examples on pages 10–11 and see if you can decide what sort of audience each one is aimed at. Put your answers in the third column of the grid you made for these texts and head it 'audience'.

5 *Leaflet*

Looking at purpose

Next, you need to decide why the media text was produced – what is its purpose? And is it trying to achieve its purpose by appealing to particular emotions?

A text could aim to:
- express feelings (e.g. the words to a love song)
- explain something (e.g. a non-fiction book)
- entertain (e.g. a TV sitcom)
- persuade (e.g. an advert)
- inform (e.g. a weather forecast).

And it could try to achieve its aim by making its audience feel:
- amused
- anxious
- envious
- any other emotion.

A radio pop music programme aims to entertain people by: amusing them with jokes and chat, informing them with snippets of news, and playing music to give them pleasure.

So to define the purpose of a text, ask these two questions:

1 What is this text trying to do?

2 What is it trying to make its audience think and feel, in order to do this?

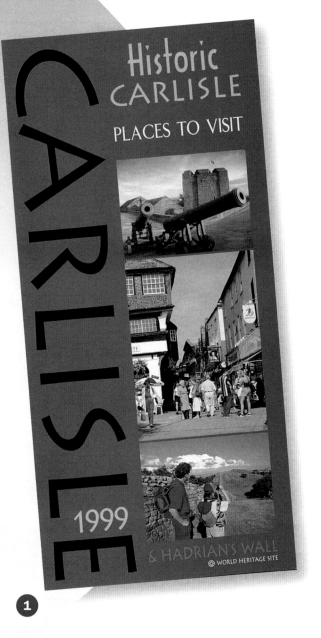

2 *Feature film*

EXCLUSIVE SEAT UPGRADE OFFER

CATS
NEW LONDON THEATRE
0171 405 0072

Les Misérables
PALACE THEATRE
0171 434 0909

Miss Saigon
THEATRE ROYAL DRURY LANE
0171 494 5000

**BUY A TICKET FOR £25.00
TO SEE ANY OF THE ABOVE WEST END SHOWS
AND RECEIVE AN EXCLUSIVE UPGRADE
TO A TOP-PRICE SEAT (£35.00).
LIMITED ALLOCATION - BOOK NOW**

CALL THE BOX OFFICE QUOTING 'RADIO TIMES SEAT UPGRADE OFFER'

MAXIMUM FOUR TICKETS PER BOOKING.
THIS OFFER ONLY APPLIES TO MONDAY TO THURSDAY PERFORMANCES UNTIL 30 SEPTEMBER 1999.
There is a limited allocation of tickets available for this offer and all tickets are subject to availability and cannot be used in conjunction with any other offer.
ALL TELEPHONE BOOKINGS SUBJECT TO BOOKING FEE.

3

1 Look at the texts on these two pages. Try to decide what is the purpose of each one.

2 Now look back at the examples on pages 10–11: why were they produced? What is their purpose? Put your answers in the fourth column of the grid you made for these texts and head it 'purpose'.

GLOBAL VIDEO
JULY 1999

2 DAYS HIRE FOR THE PRICE OF 1 DAY

ENEMY OF THE STATE

GET IT FIRST TIME OR GET IT FREE
THAT'S THE GLOBAL GUARANTEE

4

5 *TV news programme*

Looking at effectiveness

Once you have thought about the type of text, its audience and what it is trying to achieve, there is another important question to ask:

Do you think it would work?

Remember, the effect of a message is often not what the sender intended. For example an expensive film may be a flop at the box office – or a record release may not sell many copies. Sometimes, you can remember that an advert was funny, but not what it was trying to sell: so it has worked in one way, but it hasn't really achieved its purpose.

To think about effectiveness, you need to 'step back' from a media text and think about what effect it is likely to have on its audience – whether you think it would work.

▽

Look back at the examples on pages 10–11 one last time. Do you think each one would achieve its purpose? If so, why? If not, why not?

Put your answers in the fifth column of the grid you made for these texts and head it 'effectiveness'.

You've now covered the main points you need to consider when looking at any media text.

TAPE

Type:
What type of text is this?
What codes does it use?

Audience:
Who is the audience?
(Age? Gender? Interests?)

Purpose:
What is the text trying to do?
What is it trying to make its audience think and feel, in order to do this?

Effectiveness:
Do you think the text would achieve its purpose?

You can use these key questions to start analysing any media text. Look back at the notes you've put in your grid. You'll see you have already written something about the type, audience, purpose and effectiveness of each text on pages 10–11 – so you've already done your first TAPE analysis.

▼

Look again at your grid and compare your answers with a partner's. What are the similarities? What are the differences? Remember, if you've written something different, that doesn't necessarily mean that either of you is wrong – because we are individuals, we don't all read texts in exactly the same way.

Now you have a way of starting to examine media texts, we will look in more detail at the signs that make up the different codes from which texts are constructed.

You will learn how to examine how a text is constructed from signs, and how the choice of signs is affected by the type of text, its audience, and its purpose – as well as thinking about whether it is effective or not.

The code of still graphic images

An **image** is a picture.

It might be in your mind (a mental image).

It might be a moving image, as in a film.

It might be a still image, such as a photograph or drawing.

In this unit we are looking at still images.

The word **graphic** refers to the way the image is created.
It might be drawn, painted, produced by a computer or a still
camera. Still graphic images are used widely in media texts.

> ▽
>
> What media texts use still graphic images? List as
> many different types of text as you can think of.

As with any other media code, when we look at a picture, we
are reading signs. But in the case of pictures, we can often read
them so rapidly that we don't realize we are in fact 'reading'.

The knowledge you already have

You already know a lot about
the code of still graphic images.
Here are some still graphic
images taken from a range of
media texts.

1

For each example, answer the following questions:

a What does the image show?

b What type of text would the image have come from?

c Who is the likely audience for the image?

d What is the purpose that the image is being used for?

e What was it about each image which helped you decide about the purpose and audience?

Learning zone

Composition: putting messages in pictures

What is placed within the frame of a graphic image is very carefully selected and positioned. This process is called **composition**. The composition of pictures used in adverts is thought out in great detail, with attention to every object, every figure and every aspect of the setting.

A news photograph is also composed through
- the way the photograph is shot
- the way it may be manipulated during the editing process.

How do you read this image? For each of the questions below, write down the signs in the frame which give you your answer. The signs might be clothing, objects, the way people look, their gestures, etc.

a First, where do you think this scene is taking place? (Which country? In a town or in the countryside?)

b What would you say is happening in the picture?

c Would you say that this is a real event, photographed while it happened, or an event that has been posed for the camera? Say why you think this.

These two images from holiday brochures have been carefully composed. Look at the way the figures are positioned. Look at their expressions and gestures. Notice the objects within the frame and the setting for the pictures.

Now look at each picture in turn and see if you can answer the questions.

▼

The models here have been posed looking up at the camera smiling. The woman wears sunglasses and gold bracelets. The man holds an umbrella, and the girl holds a beach ball. We see them from above.

a What type of audience is this image aimed at?

b What messages about the holiday is the image sending by the way it has been composed?

1

▼

Here the models are posed differently – they are looking at each other, not at the camera. There are no objects in the frame apart from the air-beds. The woman has one arm resting on the man's back. No other people are in the frame.

a Who is the audience for this image?

b Why has the photo been taken with the two people facing towards each other rather than towards the camera?

c What is the difference in the way this picture is trying to appeal to its audience, compared to the other picture?

d Write a caption for each picture which might persuade people to book the sort of holiday it represents.

2

Composition can be broken down into different elements. Now we'll look at various elements of composition in more detail.

Figure signs

Almost all still graphic images feature human figures. In all graphic images except news photographs, these figures are likely to have been deliberately posed in some way. The way they are posed can affect how you read the picture – so it is important to examine how human figures are used in pictures.

- How are the figures sitting, standing, moving?

- What emotions are they showing through their facial expressions and body language?

- How are they dressed?

- How are they positioned in relation to other figures or objects in the frame?

You already know how to 'read' people. You do it every day. You read facial expressions, body language, hand gestures. Someone raises a fist – you know it means anger. Someone frowns – you know they're puzzled.

Now apply your knowledge to figure signs in pictures. Look at the images here and think about reading them.

Face signs

These include all facial expressions – shape of mouth, shape of eyes (e.g. narrowed, wide-eyed), direction of gaze, eyebrows (raised in surprise, lowered in a frown), etc.

> ▽
>
> For each image on this page, write down words which would describe the feelings of the person or people shown.

Hand signs

People use their hands to express feelings too. These pictures show just some of the range of hand signs that you use every day, and which can be used in still graphic images.

2

1

3

4

▽

1 Look at the various hand signs on this page. Write down the message each hand sign is sending about how the person feels.

2 With a partner, discuss and demonstrate what you would do with your hands if you were feeling:

a afraid

b caring

c powerful

d confused

e friendly.

Now write a description of these hand signs.

Body signs

These include all aspects of body appearance:

- posture – how a person stands, sits, how they position their hands, feet, arms, head, etc.

- dress – includes clothing, jewellery, etc.

- hair – colour, style.

1

2

▽

1 Try reading these two pictures.

  a What can you tell about the woman in each picture from her hair-style, the way she is dressed, and the objects around her?

  b Write down three words to describe each woman's feelings.

  c What is it about each woman's body posture and facial expression which tells you about her feelings?

2 With a partner, discuss and demonstrate the body posture which might convey the following feelings:
  a tiredness
  b anger
  c shyness
  d terror
  e grief.

Now describe each posture in words.

Shape and proportion

Look for the way outlines and shapes of things are used in pictures. Does the shape look natural or unnatural? Shapes can be made to look unnatural by showing parts of them out of proportion: too big or too small by comparison to the rest of the image.

Look at these representations of dinosaurs. Each one has been drawn to suit a particular audience and purpose.

Shapes can also be changed to create a specific effect – to create humour or fear, for example.

In this cartoon, look at the body shapes of the two politicians Tony Blair and William Hague. Look at the expressions on their faces, and the way each of them is standing.

'Game Blair. Hague to serve'

▼

Compare the pictures of dinosaurs.

a Write down some of the differences in the ways the dinosaurs have been drawn.

b What audience do you think each image is aimed at? Give reasons for your answer.

▼

a What is happening in the picture? Why do you think the cartoonist has used the setting of a tennis match?

b What is the difference in the way the two politicians are presented?

c How is the reader meant to feel towards each of them?

Colour, texture, and lighting

These graphic signs are used to affect the mood and atmosphere of the image. They affect our impressions of what is happening within the frame. Smooth, even textures create a different feeling from rough, uneven textures. For example, using the setting of a smooth, calm sea for an advert creates a very different atmosphere from a rough, stormy sea.

Colours act as powerful signs to affect our emotions. Red and purple are strong colours, while pink is more gentle. Using light and dark shades also affects our feelings – bright, sunny images make us feel different from dark, shadowy pictures.

Look at the way colour, texture and lighting have been used in these two media texts.

The Dorset leaflet is a blend of images (called photo-montage) all shot in bright sunlight, whereas the Zelda advert is full of shadows. The Dorset leaflet uses lots of bright colours, while the Zelda advert's colours are mostly dark and subdued.

▽

a What mood and atmosphere are created by the use of colour and lighting in each text?

b Can you list three different textures used in the Zelda advert?

c Who do you think is the audience for each text and what is its purpose? How do you think the use of lighting, colour and texture relates to this?

Viewpoint

Viewpoint is the position from which we seem to view an image. It might be from **close-up** or a **long shot**. It might also be from a **high level** or a **low level**, from in front of the subject or behind.

A close-up can be used to make the reader feel more involved; a long shot can make the reader feel more detached.

A low-level viewpoint looks up at the subject from below. This can make the subject of the image seem dominant and powerful.

A high-level viewpoint looks down on the subject. It can be used to give a general view of something, and can make the reader feel less involved.

Here are two images of canoeing. One is a close-up with a low-level viewpoint. The other is a long shot, from a high-level viewpoint.

A high-level viewpoint might make the reader feel less involved, but it can also give more information about what is happening. The long shot of the canoeist shows you the danger of the situation and is exciting in a different way from the close-up.

'Tilting' the reader's viewpoint is also a technique used by graphic artists and photographers to give a feeling of energy and movement to an image. This use of diagonals contrasts with the use of the more normal horizontal viewpoint which always feels more natural and calm.

1

▽

1 Look at these two pictures of cars.

  a Which picture is taken from a high-level viewpoint? Which is from a low-level viewpoint?

  b Which picture is a close-up? Which is a long shot?

  c Does either of the images use a diagonal tilt?

  d How does the use of viewpoint affect the atmosphere of the images? What does it suggest about each car?

2 Imagine you are working on an advertising brochure featuring the two car photographs. Make a list of key words that each picture brings to your mind. Then work in a group with your lists of key words, to come up with an advertising slogan or caption for each picture.

2

The reader's response to a photograph of people can be strongly influenced by whose point of view is represented.

The three images below all show conflict between police and protesters, but from different viewpoints.

▼

> Look at each image in turn and say how the viewpoint affects your feelings towards
> a the police
> b the protesters.

A news photograph is always given a caption to 'anchor' its meaning. Several newspapers may use the same picture. But if they use different captions, they may change the way you read (understand) the picture.

▼

> 1 Look again at picture 1. Here are two possible captions:
>
>   A Police battle to restore law and order.
>   B Riot police show no mercy for protesters.
>
>   How would caption A make you feel towards the police, and towards the protesters? And caption B?
>
> 2 Now write two captions for each of the other two pictures:
>   a to make the reader sympathize with the police.
>   b to make the reader sympathize with the protesters.

1

2

3

The impact of news photographs

Powerful photographs or pictures can stay in the memory for a very long time.

Here is an award-winning photograph, taken during the war in Kosovo in 1999 by *Observer* photographer Andrew Testa. The picture focuses on two Albanian refugees, a mother and child, forcibly removed from their home in Kosovo.

Study the picture carefully for a few moments.

1 Write down exactly what you can see. Where are these people? How old are they? What are they doing? What are they wearing? Describe their gestures and expressions. (This process of detailed looking is called **denotation**.)

2 Now move on to explore what this picture might mean to you. (This process of thinking about meanings is called **connotation**.)

a How does this picture affect your thoughts and feelings? Write down words which come into your head when you look at this picture.

b This mother and child are refugees. Are they the same as or different from your idea of 'refugees'? Give reasons for your answer.

c What do the gestures of the mother and child tell you about their possible feelings? What might the child be saying to her mother?

d Why do you think this picture won an award? What is special or unusual about it?

You now know something about how pictures are constructed to convey messages. You have seen the way various graphic signs are used to signify the message to an audience.

You're now going to use what you've just learned to deconstruct (take apart) some picture messages to reveal how they have been put together.

To help you do this, you're going to use a process called **two-step reading**. This is a way of slowing down the way we examine a media text so that we can study it more closely. (In fact, you've just tried out this process in the questions about the Kosovo refugees picture.)

You can use two-step reading to examine any type of media text.

> **Checklist of graphic signs**
>
> Figure signs
>   *Face signs*
>   *Hand signs*
>   *Body signs*
> Shape, proportion
> Colour, texture, lighting
> Viewpoint

Two-step reading

Step one (denotation)

First just make a note of what is there.

With a picture text, note the use of human figures and objects, and the uses of viewpoint, shape, proportion, colour, texture and lighting.

This process is called **denotation**: you're denoting (describing) the signs that are in the text.

Step two (connotation)

Now try to explain the effect the various signs have on you.

What ideas or feelings come into your mind when you look at, for example, the colours, the lighting, and the gestures used by the people in the image?

These ideas and feelings are called **connotations**.

The graphic image text on page 33 has been deconstructed using a simple form of two-step reading, to show how some of the various graphic signs have been used.

First, each particular feature or graphic sign is described (denotation).

Then, in italics, there is a note on what the sign might be intended to mean, or what its effect might be on the reader (connotation).

Colour:
deep red background = *rising sun, Japan, drama, danger*

Shape:
horns on helmet = *devilish, threatening, powerful*

Figure, gesture:
sword raised, pointing forwards = *threatening, dangerous*

Colour, texture:
black metallic armour = *hard, sinister*

Colour, lighting:
normal daylight: contrasts with exotic colours at top of leaflet = *allows reader to identify with roller-coaster riders*

Viewpoint:
high-level, slightly tilted, approaching reader = *creates excitement and sense of movement*

Colour, shape:
black silhouette of ride = *sinister, spooky, like a spider*

Colour, gesture:
red staring eyes = *devilish, threatening*

Viewpoint:
figure at eye level, face to face = *aggressive, threatening*

Viewpoint:
tiger face to face at eye level = *dramatic, powerful*

Figure, gesture:
small child with tiger face make-up, hands like claws = *playful, fun, appealing to young children and parents*

Figure, gesture:
Young people dressed in summer clothes, mouths open, arms raised = *sense of fun, excitement, appealing to young people*

▽

Now look at the following image.

The first stage of two-step reading has been done for you – various graphic signs have been picked out and described (denotation).

1 You must do the second step. See if you can decide what effect each of the graphic signs is intended to have on the reader, and make a note of it. This is the second step of two-step reading (connotation). To get you started, some connotations have been done already.

2 Look at the list you have compiled and compare your thoughts with other pupils. What overall impression is the reader meant to get of this comic book character?

3 Summarize your comments on this image, using the TAPE questions.

TAPE

Type:
What type of text is this?
What codes does it use?

Audience:
Who is the audience?
(Age? Gender? Interests?)

Purpose:
What is the text trying to do? What is it trying to make its audience think and feel, in order to do this?

Effectiveness:
Do you think the text would achieve its purpose?

Comic book image

A **Texture:** hard, metallic, shiny =

B **Shape:** sharp eagle head and talons =

C **Figure:** unseen eyes = *threatening, insensitive*

D **Colour:** black, with jagged line like lightning bolt =

E **Figure, gesture:** square jaw, unsmiling mouth =

F **Colour, texture:** ribbed, black/metallic jacket =

G **Shape:** chain-link zipper = *strong, unbreakable, suggests law and order, locking people up*

H **Gesture:** hand gripping belt =

I **Viewpoint:** viewer is placed on eye level of figure, face-to-face =

J **Colour:** yellow/gold = *wealth, high position, authority*

K **Shape:** helmet and shoulder armour =

L **Texture:** glassy, metallic knuckle armour =

M **Colour, lighting:** out of focus background, paler than figure = *makes lines of figure harder and sharper*

Task zone

Deconstruction tasks

Now's your chance to test your knowledge. There are four graphic texts for you to deconstruct. Try to do as many as you can. Two are shown on these pages. Two – the Dorset Attractions leaflet and Zelda advert – are on pages 26–27.

Checklist of graphic signs

Figure signs
 Face signs
 Hand signs
 Body signs
Shape, proportion
Colour, texture, lighting
Viewpoint

For each image, use two-step reading, and sum up with the TAPE questions.

a Denotation: describe what is in the frame, referring to the graphic signs being used.

b Connotation: say what you think each sign is intended to mean.

c Summary: use the TAPE key questions to give your final comments, saying:

Type
What type of text is this?
What codes does it use?

Audience
Who is the audience?
(Age? Gender? Interests?)

Purpose
What is the text trying to do?
What is it trying to make its audience think and feel, in order to do this?

Effectiveness
Do you think the text would achieve its purpose?

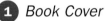

1 *Book Cover*

The Tower at
MOONVILLE

STEPHEN ELBOZ

Dorset Attractions leaflet
(page 26)

 Zelda advert
(page 27)

 City break promotion

You now have to construct your own graphic images, using the knowledge of graphic signs that you have gained in this unit.

Construction task 1

You are competing with others in the class to win the contract for a publicity campaign. You must produce ideas for a series of eight images to promote your town or region for visitors.

Purpose: to persuade and inform
Audience: there are two audiences:

a families with teenage children
b retired people.

You must construct four frames of graphic images for each audience.

Use large sheets of plain paper. Draw the four frames for each audience.

Sketch what will go in each frame and give accompanying notes to explain the details of the composition of each frame. Your notes should indicate how you are using graphic signs, and why you feel your images will have the right effect on your audience.

You may be asked to present your ideas to the rest of the class. Your teacher will judge who wins the contract.

You can use the TAPE questions to help you think about key issues, or to structure your presentation:

Type
What type of text am I constructing? What codes can I use?

Audience
Who is it aimed at?

Purpose
What is it trying to do? How shall I try to do this? (How do I want the audience to feel? How can I use signs to get this response?)

Effectiveness
Will it work? (Show a friend, check it out and change bits if necessary.)

Checklist of graphic signs

Figure signs
   Face signs
   Hand signs
   Body signs
Shape, proportion
Colour, texture, lighting
Viewpoint

Construction task 2

Individual project or group display

Make a collection from newspapers and magazines of images to illustrate all the graphic signs you've learnt about in this unit.

The code of written language

The knowledge you already have

You already know a lot about the code of written language. Find out by looking at these texts.

▽

Test yourself on the texts, using the TAPE key questions:

Type
What type of text is this?
What codes does it use?

Audience
Who is the audience?
(Age Gender? Interests?)

Purpose
What is this text trying to do?
What is it trying to make its audience think and feel, in order to achieve this purpose?

Effectiveness
Do you think the text would achieve its purpose?

Now we will look in more detail at how written language texts are constructed.

1

Internet whizz-kid **Tom Hadfield is on-line to become one of the country's richest teenagers – at 16.**

The computer genius has already tapped into his first million after starting the football website Soccernet. He was only 12 when he launched the service by emailing football results around the word as they appeared on Teletext.

2

Re-enter the Gecko

Okay, so the new Gex game has you drooooling with excitement (close your mouth there, you're dribbling! At least catch it in a cup! Yeurk!), but what about the original? Even though it's a year old now, which is about 612 in videogame years, *Enter the Gecko* is still a pretty tidy platformer.

3

Win £10,000 *in vouchers and cash!*

Can you imagine the thrill of winning £10,000 in vouchers and cash? You'd be out that door and down the shops quicker than you can say 'Yippee!' Clothes, holidays, jewellery, furniture, food and booze... all could be yours. So don't dream it – go for it today!

4

Jamaica's Ultimate Indulgence

Nestling oceanside in Ocho Rios, a one-of-a-kind, history-rich treasure called Villa Rio Chico invites discerning guests to its fourteen acres of rivers, streams, waterfalls, private pools, Roman gardens, cove beaches, and gracious seclusion. Join a privileged few for an all-inclusive masterpiece holiday with a chef who will conjure your fantasies...

Learning zone

Written language is a code made up of word and letter signs. It also uses a range of devices and techniques which convey meaning and can affect a reader's thoughts and feelings. Here, we will look at some of the signs and devices that can be used to construct a written language text.

Alliteration

Alliteration can give a punchy sound if strong consonant sounds are used:

It can also give a more gentle sound if softer consonant sounds are used:

> **Alliteration:**
> using words close together which begin with the same consonant sound

BOYS RESCUED FROM BURNING BOAT

Try this simple soothing soap, so kind to your skin.

▽

Write two sentences using alliteration. In the first use strong consonant sounds. In the second use more gentle consonant sounds.

Assonance

Assonance can be used to create emphasis or for humorous effect:

> **Assonance:**
> using words close together which contain the same vowel sounds

Michael Owen goes for broke

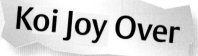

Koi Joy Over

▽

Write two sentences using assonance.

Product names – the power of alliteration and assonance

Because of the catchy sound created by alliteration and assonance, product names often use these techniques.

Adjective tag

Adjective tags are often used in news stories to convey information quickly. The adjective tag could be made up of a single adjective or an adjectival phrase. (An adjectival phrase uses several words to describe a subject.)

Look at the following examples. The adjective tags are highlighted.

> 1 Where are alliteration and assonance used in these product names?
>
> a Kit Kat
> b Coca Cola
> c Tetley Tea
> d Fruit 'n' Fibre
> e Pritt Stick
> f Curly Wurly
>
> 2 Can you write down five more product names which use alliteration and/or assonance?

> **Adjective tag:**
> adding an adjective (a word which describes a person or thing) to the name of a person

Mother of three Joyce Henderson won £1 million on the lottery

Ace goal-scorer Terry Wright had a brilliant game for United

Handsome Ricky Turner struck lucky yesterday

> Write a sentence using an adjective tag describing someone in your class who achieves success at something.

Rhyme

Using words which rhyme can give a catchy 'feel' to language. It's a technique often used in advertising jingles and newspaper headlines:

> Use rhyme in an advertising jingle or slogan for a new food or drink product.

A Mars a day helps you work rest and play.

Hero Jimmy has gotta lotta bottle.

Emotive language

Some words are like fireworks – they explode with emotions. They may be pleasant or unpleasant feelings. Media writers often use emotive language:

The Prince watched a dazzling display of brilliant gymnastics...

In Kosovo the full horror of these appalling events was seen...

> **Emotive language:** words and phrases which cause strong feelings in the reader

---

1 Look at these two pieces of writing. Write down the emotive words or phrases used in them.

2 Now re-read both texts. Who do you think is the audience for each one? What is the purpose of the texts?

A

SCENIC FRANCE

The small picturesque town of St. Augustine nestles in the hills near Limoges. With its quaint cobbled streets and friendly bars, this rural beauty spot draws tourists from far and wide. In summer, the streets are adorned with cascades of brilliant flowers, and lively street artists add a unique charm and magic to this quiet French backwater.

SACKED BOY'S RIFLE RAMPAGE

A gun-crazy teenager mowed down over 30 of his former school-mates yesterday in Springfield, Oregon. Expelled the previous day, the 16 year old sought revenge in a mindless display of appalling violence, killing one and injuring 30 others. The bravery of one of the wrestling team ended the mayhem when the boy was brought down and disarmed.

B

Opinion or fact? The effect of emotive language

One of the difficulties in decoding written information is separating fact from opinion. Facts are those statements which can be proved to be true. Opinions are someone's personal views.

In newspaper reports you have to check carefully whether a statement is a fact or an opinion. Often the opinions are cleverly hidden. One of the clues to look out for is the use of emotive words.

Look at these two statements:

Shearer played as striker for England.

Shearer played superbly as striker for England.

The first statement is fact. The second statement is opinion. The addition of the emotive word 'superbly' makes the difference, as it carries the opinion of the writer.

Puns

A

Why did the boy take a hammer to school at the end of term?

Because it was breaking-up day.

B

How many ears did Star Trek's Captain Kirk have?

Three – a left ear, a right ear, and space the final frontier.

These jokes both rely on puns. A pun is where a word is used to suggest two different meanings at once (joke A) or because it sounds like a word with a different meaning (joke B). A pun teases you as you try to work out the two meanings.

Puns are often used in newspaper headlines to grab the reader's attention:

COOL CATHY CHILLS OUT AFTER FROZEN LAKE RESCUE

Schoolgirl Cathy saved a young boy from drowning after he fell through the ice

Cool and *chills out* are used here because they have a connection with cold things (like the frozen lake) as well as having specific meanings: Cathy is *cool* because she is a heroine; she *chills out* or relaxes now her rescue work is done.

▼

1 Write down a statement of fact, then change it to an opinion by adding an emotive word.

2 Read the texts on page 42 again, and think about the emotive words they use. What is the opinion of the writer about their subject in each case?

▼

1 Read the following examples and work out the double meanings.

WATER WAY TO WED

A diving-mad bride and groom took the plunge yesterday and became the first couple in Britain to take their vows in an underwater ceremony.

COPS AND ROBERTS

Villain Archie Roberts caught in the nick of time

2 Write down a joke with a pun in it. Can you make up a punning joke of your own too?

3 Try to find four examples of newspaper headlines that use puns. The sports section of Sunday papers is a good place to start looking. See if you can explain how the puns work.

Syntax and rhythm

Syntax includes such things as word order and length of sentences. Syntax affects the 'feel' and rhythm of a piece of writing: for example, short sentences can create a lively, dramatic mood, while longer sentences can create a more relaxed mood.

Texts A and B are both taken from holiday brochures. The purpose of each piece is to persuade.

Syntax:

how words go together to make up sentences

Text A

MAKE MINE IBIZA!

Ibiza is it! **Great** beaches, cool hotels. **Sizzling** eating, **explosive** night life. **Sun-soaked** sand, cool sea.

Life's a **party** in Ibiza.

Grab a cold one and make for the **heat**!

Make Mine Ibiza!

Text B

GO GREEK AND FEEL THE DIFFERENCE

There's something about Greece which is hard to define. Maybe it's the exquisite clarity of the light, the eternal blueness of sea and sky, the scatterings of tavernas spilling out on to the sand. It's a country to explore for its rich history, for its vibrant colour and its people whose love of life is legendary...

Try using **two-step reading** (see page 32) on these two texts.

1 **Denotation**
(noting what is there)

a What is each text about?

b Count the number of sentences in texts A and B. Then count the number of words in each sentence. How many words are in the longest and the shortest sentences in each text?

c List the emotive words and phrases in each text.

2 **Connotation**
(meanings and effects)

a Which of the following adjectives would you use to describe the rhythm of each text?

lively relaxed tranquil calm exciting peaceful gentle vigorous vibrant

b What audience is text A aimed at? What audience is text B aimed at?

c How is the syntax of each text used to appeal to the target audience?

Using syntax

Try this activity to see if you can use syntax to create an appropriate rhythm for two different audiences.

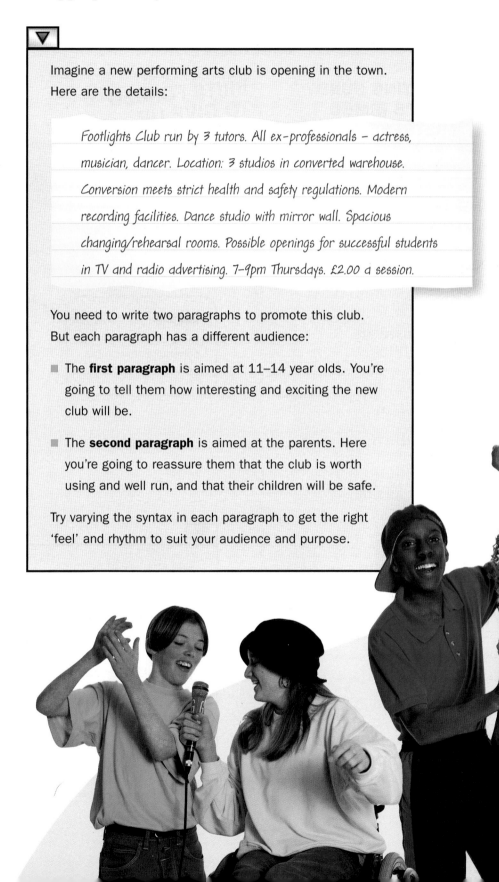

Imagine a new performing arts club is opening in the town. Here are the details:

> *Footlights Club run by 3 tutors. All ex-professionals – actress, musician, dancer. Location: 3 studios in converted warehouse. Conversion meets strict health and safety regulations. Modern recording facilities. Dance studio with mirror wall. Spacious changing/rehearsal rooms. Possible openings for successful students in TV and radio advertising. 7–9pm Thursdays. £2.00 a session.*

You need to write two paragraphs to promote this club. But each paragraph has a different audience:

■ The **first paragraph** is aimed at 11–14 year olds. You're going to tell them how interesting and exciting the new club will be.

■ The **second paragraph** is aimed at the parents. Here you're going to reassure them that the club is worth using and well run, and that their children will be safe.

Try varying the syntax in each paragraph to get the right 'feel' and rhythm to suit your audience and purpose.

Slang or chatty language

This is also called colloquial language. Using it can give a fast, slick tone to the writing. In addition, slang words are used in newspaper headlines because they are often short and punchy.

In the following examples, the slang words are highlighted.

'DON'T SACK US GUV' SAY WORKERS

CHEATING HUBBY DUMPS BIMBO MISTRESS

BRITS FORCED TO GIVE UP HOLS IN SPAIN

▼

Use slang in a newspaper headline for a report about a burglar who hid stolen goods in a disused public lavatory.

Imagery

The most common types of imagery used are simile, metaphor and personification.

A **simile** is when one thing is compared to something else using the word 'like' or 'as':

Left-winger Johnny Burns raced past three defenders like a tornado.

This shampoo leaves your hair as soft as silk.

A **metaphor** is a more powerful image where one thing is described as if it actually is something else:

The full-back was a tower of strength.

The teacher fired questions at the class.

Personification is a type of metaphor where something non-human is given human qualities:

The engine in the ZR5 model has real muscle.

The colour will leap out and grab you.

Imagery:
words which create a powerful picture in the mind of the reader

Use imagery to describe:

a the colour or taste of a soft drink (use a simile)

b a goal being scored in a football match (use a metaphor)

c a stormy night (use personification).

Active and passive voice

A 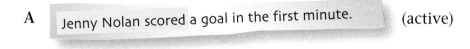 Jenny Nolan scored a goal in the first minute.   (active)

B   A goal was scored in the first minute by Jenny Nolan.   (passive)

The active voice draws attention to the person carrying out an action. It is more personal and can be more dramatic. Sentence A focuses on Jenny and what she did.

The passive voice draws attention to the action, rather than the person doing it. It is more impersonal. Sentence B focuses on the goal, not Jenny.

The tone of a technical or factual account often needs to be impersonal, so the passive can be more appropriate there:

> **Active and passive voice:** different forms of the verb which reveal or disguise who is doing the action in a sentence

C   The Titan rocket was launched at midday by Mission Control.   (passive)

D   Mission Control launched the Titan rocket at midday.   (active)

C is more appropriate here – the reader is not really interested in who launched the rocket.

▼

1 Which of the following sentences use the active voice and which use the passive voice?

  a The fire was started by a group of twelve year olds.
  b The match was attended by fifty thousand enthusiastic fans.
  c The Mayor opened the summer fair at midday.
  d The bomb was detonated by political extremists yesterday.
  e Mrs Jensen chased a neighbour down the street.
  f The young mother was knocked down by the drunken driver.

2 Now re-write each sentence changing those written with the active voice to passive voice and vice versa.

Imperative verbs

Imperative verbs are often used in adverts.
The verb generally starts the sentence or phrase:

> **Imperative verbs:**
> verbs which tell the reader to do something

Get active. Take regular exercise.

BUY ONE, GET ONE FREE!

Don't delay – book early to avoid disappointment.

Interrogative verbs

Media writers use interrogative verbs to ask persuasive questions. These are called **rhetorical questions** and they are designed to make the reader sit up and take notice:

> **Interrogative verbs:**
> verbs which ask questions, including rhetorical questions

Are you still having problems with dandruff?

When did you last change your engine oil?

Are you waiting for the man of your dreams?

1 Can you spot the use of imperative and interrogative verbs in the following paragraph? Write down the words or phrases which use these techniques.

   Thinking about the summer? Are you having problems keeping the kids happy? Can't make up your mind where to go? Come on down to Pinkerton's Travel Bureau. We have all the answers. Don't delay. Give us a ring or better still, call in. We'll give you the holiday of a lifetime.

2 Now write a paragraph to tell middle-aged people about the importance of taking regular exercise. Try to use both imperative and interrogative verbs in your writing. You could mention: improving circulation, avoiding heart disease, relieving stress, living longer, enjoying life, having more energy, working more efficiently.

Representation and bias

The way people, places and events are represented in media texts is a key feature you should look out for. In newspapers, for example, people and events may be represented in a very biased way to try to influence the readers' opinions. Newspaper writers may use a variety of language signs to represent a person or event in a way which is heavily biased. This process of giving a biased representation is sometimes called giving an event 'spin'.

Read these two representations of the same event:

A

A small group of hunt protesters voiced their protest as a red-faced hunt master scurried towards the safety of police lines.

B

A scruffy bunch of hunt saboteurs screamed obscenities as the hunt master rode calmly towards the police lines.

1 In which of these versions is the representation biased:

 a against the hunt master and in favour of the protesters?

 b against the protesters and in favour of the hunt master?

2 Pick out the words in the two versions which carry:

 a positive connotations

 b negative connotations.

3 Why have the writers used these words – what are they trying to make the reader feel about the hunt master and the protesters in each sentence?

Looking at newspapers

Of all the types of printed media, such as newspapers, books, magazines and brochures, the type people most often read is the newspaper. As well as the language signs we have discussed so far, newspapers also have some special features which we will look at over the next few pages.

Headlines, captions and other tricks of presentation

Writers who create media texts use a range of what are called 'presentational devices' to grab the attention of an audience. On a newspaper page – or an advert, leaflet or poster – the arrangement of words and lettering can make the difference between holding and losing a reader's attention.

Some of the presentational devices used in newspapers are illustrated below.

Bold large print headline

Sub-heading underlined

Opening paragraph in bold print

Fonts on logo irregular and informal to give 'fun' feel

Coloured logo tilted to create sense of energy/movement

Key words in bold capital letters

Bold type to draw attention

White on black print – arrow shape to draw attention

Bullet point to draw attention

Use of colour to draw attention

33,000 SCHOOLS   2 BILLION TOKENS   MILLIONS OF BOOKS

A TOKEN OF OUR ESTEEM FOR JO

Her collection totals 5,000

WHIZZKID Joanne Mumford has gathered an amazing 5,500 Books for Schools tokens – making her a Sun Super Collector.

The 12-year-old's feat earns her a Sun certificate and will bring 55 free books for her school, **HERNE BAY HIGH**, Kent.

Joanne got off to a flying start by using her home computer to print notices about the scheme.

Her dad David stuck them up around Kent University in Canterbury where he works as a porter.

Mum Sharon says: 'The students have given hundreds of tokens. Joanne has also made sure every relative has changed their newspaper to The Sun.

'She searches litter bins for tokens and we have to follow people to get their tokens if we see someone eating a bag of Walkers crisps.'

Joanne says: 'I just can't collect tokens fast enough.'

Another high-scoring collector is Keiron Gathercorne, seven, who has amassed 1,500 tokens for **GLADE PRIMARY SCHOOL** in Suffolk.

His mum Debbie brings them home from the factory where she works. And Avon Lady Kerry Lyons got 2,500 tokens for Glade Primary by recruiting customers to help.

● HALF the pupils studying for GCSEs are not given the textbooks they need to help them pass exams, says a survey from Keele University, Staffs.

KEEP cutting out tokens – today's is on the right.
DO you know a Super Collector who has found an unusual way to boost their school's token total?
Call us today on 0171 782 4021 from 9am to 6pm.

TODAY'S TOKEN

The five Ws rule of newspaper reporting

In the opening paragraphs of any news report, the writer generally aims to answer the following questions:

Who?   Who was involved?

What?   What happened?

When?   When did the event happen?

Where?   Where did it happen

Why?   Why and how did the event happen?

▽

Re-read the report on page 50 and see how many of the five Ws it answers. Pick out words or phrases which answer each question.

▽

Now read this article from the *Sun* newspaper. Try to answer the following questions and give examples of the features you find.

a Can you find the five Ws? How many of them does this article use?

b What presentation features does this article have?

c Can you find some examples of alliteration?

d Can you find any puns?

e Can you find some examples of chatty language or slang?

f Are the verbs mostly active or passive? Give examples.

FAME BID BY GUM

TOOTHLESS trumpeter Alan Hammond is hoping to make a sucker of the music business with a novel way to toot his horn.

The wacky 66-year-old, of Cayton, North Yorkshire, sucks and blows the instrument after losing all but five of his teeth. He hopes to find fame as a novelty act on TV shows such as TFI Friday or Barrymore.

Broadsheet and tabloid newspapers

Newspapers can be divided into two main categories: broadsheet and tabloid. Broadsheet newspapers include the *Times*, the *Telegraph*, the *Guardian* and the *Independent*. Tabloids include the *Daily Mirror*, the *Sun*, the *Daily Express*, and the *Daily Mail*.

Broadsheet

> Look at the two front pages.
>
> a Which paper has the most words?
>
> b Which devotes the most space to pictures?
>
> c Which has the largest headlines?
>
> d Which looks as if it will be easier to understand?
>
> e Which looks most serious?

Tabloid

The different papers are constructed with their specific audiences in mind. The writers know what their audience will expect.

Typical broadsheet readers will expect:	Typical tabloid readers will expect:
detailed, factual, unbiased reporting	reports which are entertaining as well as informative, and which may be dramatic and sensational
issues to be dealt with seriously	a mixture of serious and light-hearted topics
complex language which uses a wide vocabulary	language which is easy to read
more space on a page given to printed text than to pictures	more space on a page given to pictures than printed text

Imogen's a bubbly bike babe

By SEAN O'BRIEN

MOTORBIKE-mad Imogen Whitaker wears a leather jacket, oily jeans, heavy black boots, rides a 750cc Suzuki... and runs her own French champagne house!

She and boyfriend Didier Pierson have produced their own vintages for four years from their idyllic chateau at Avize in Champagne province.

Ex-teacher Imogen, 40, of Pinner in Middlesex, met champagne taster Didier, a fellow biker, when she was touring with her club.

His machine had crashed so she hauled him aboard hers. Romance and a new career soon brewed for her.

Locals reckon their champagne is grape stuff.

Tabloid article

Teachers defiant on holiday cuts

Rebecca Smithers

TEACHERS yesterday underlined their determination to hang on to their last significant perk – the long summer holiday – as for the first time they threatened industrial action over radical plans by a number of local authorities for a five-term academic year.

Nigel de Gruchy, general secretary of the National Union of Schoolmasters Union of Women Teachers, said there was a very 'real possibility' that his members would boycott any such arrangements by refusing to work to the new timetable.

A growing number of local authorities – including a group of Labour-controlled London councils – have drawn up plans to switch to a revised academic year which would slash the six-week summer break to four weeks and shorten the length of school terms.

But yesterday teachers launched a mass protest at the NASUWT conference in Eastbourne, complaining that the new arrangements would create a longer working year for them while causing chaos for families' child care and holiday arrangements.

Broadsheet article

▽

Read the two articles, then answer these questions, to compare the style of language used in them.

a Which article seems to stick to plain facts?

b Which one uses more emotive language? Give any examples you can find.

c Which one has the most puns, alliteration, assonance, imagery, adjective tags and slang? Give examples.

d Which one has the longest sentences and paragraphs?

e Which one tries to make its story entertaining?

Here is a summary of the differences in style of language and reporting in the different kinds of newspaper.

Broadsheet	Tabloid
Little use of highly emotive words	Frequent use of emotive language
News stories written to give plain facts	News stories often written in a lively style, using devices such as puns, imagery, alliteration, assonance
Sentences can be long and complex	Sentences and paragraphs kept short
Stories are generally factual and impersonal	Stories often personal, 'human interest'; tend to use a lot of quoted speech

See how well you can analyse the next two newspaper texts.

In this first text, the main language features have been numbered.

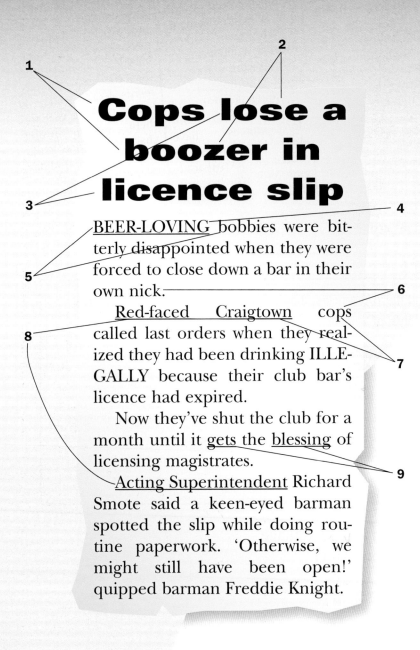

Cops lose a boozer in licence slip

BEER-LOVING bobbies were bitterly disappointed when they were forced to close down a bar in their own nick.

Red-faced Craigtown cops called last orders when they realized they had been drinking ILLEGALLY because their club bar's licence had expired.

Now they've shut the club for a month until it gets the blessing of licensing magistrates.

Acting Superintendent Richard Smote said a keen-eyed barman spotted the slip while doing routine paperwork. 'Otherwise, we might still have been open!' quipped barman Freddie Knight.

▼

a Say what language technique each number is pointing out. Then comment on what effects the writer is trying to create by using each of them. For example, 'Beer-loving bobbies' is an adjective tag, used to give information about the policemen in a little space. The alliteration and use of the slang word 'bobbies' help to make the policemen's situation sound humorous.

b Does the report include the five Ws?

c Do you think this is a tabloid or a broadsheet article? Why?

Checklist of language signs

Alliteration
Assonance
Adjective tag
Rhyme
Slang
Emotive language
Puns
Syntax/rhythm
Imagery
Active/passive voice
Imperative verbs
Interrogative verbs
Presentational devices

This newspaper article uses various language techniques to attract and entertain the reader.

RAGING GUN BATTLE TRAPS BLITZED BRITS

By GRAHAM BROUGH

HOLIDAY Brits hid in terror for two hours yesterday after a huge bomb wrecked two hotels and a machinegun battle flared outside.

The blast killed 14 people and wounded 96 – seven of them British.

Rescuers were held up on the streets of the Sri Lankan capital Colombo as Tamil Tiger gunmen and the army fought it out.

The Britons, holidaymakers and businessmen, were taken to hospital with wounds from flying glass.

The bomb, loaded on a truck, exploded in the street by the hotel at 7.15am. Tamil Tigers then attacked police with automatic weapons.

London banker John Chang, 37, who saved an injured honeymooner with makeshift bandages, said: 'It was scary. The terrorists were fighting a whole battalion. We could hear gunfire, grenades and rocket launchers really clearly for about two hours.'

Bernard Atkins, of North Ferriby, Yorks, said: 'I'm covered in about a million tiny cuts. But I'm glad to be alive. It was very frightening hearing rifle fire hitting the hotel walls.'

Three terrorists were killed after taking 20 people hostage.

Read the report, and then try to spot the reporter's use of language signs.

1 In the headline, note any examples of the following you can find: emotive words, slang, alliteration, assonance, rhyme.

2 How many paragraphs make up the report? Are they mainly long or short? What effect is created by the use of short paragraphs?

3 Now look for as many examples as you can find of the following signs in the report:
a adjective tags
b emotive words
c use of the active and passive voice

4 What effect is the writer's choice of words and language signs intended to have on the reader? Think especially about these words and phrases: *raging gun battle, blitzed Brits, an injured honeymooner, makeshift bandages.*

5 What is the journalist's purpose in writing this report? Is it simply to inform the reader of the facts?

6 Does the report answer the five Ws? Pick out words or phrases which answer each question.

Task zone

Deconstruction task 1

These two texts are the back covers of two books on the 1998 World Cup, each devised to interest a different audience.

Checklist of language signs

Alliteration
Assonance
Adjective tag
Rhyme
Slang
Emotive language
Puns
Syntax/rhythm
Imagery
Active/passive voice
Imperative verbs
Interrogative verbs
Presentational devices

Study the texts and then answer the following questions to use two-step reading:

1 Denotation
(noting what is there)
a What is the text about?
b Can you spot the use of particular language signs – for example, the use of alliteration, imagery, and emotive language? Also describe the differences in syntax/rhythm.

2 Connotation
(meanings and effects)
a What is the purpose of each of these two texts?
b Who is the audience for each text?
c Taking each text in turn, comment on the way headlines are used.
d In what ways is the syntax of each text designed to suit its audience?
e What presentational devices are used in the texts to help the reader get the message? (See page 50 for a reminder of presentational devices.)
f In your opinion, are these two texts likely to be effective with their audiences? Say why or why not.

A

OFFICIAL LICENSED PRODUCT

FIFA WORLD CUP SUPER STARS

THE WORLD CUP is the world's greatest sports spectacle. This time around, France has the honour of hosting the competition. It will be a feast of footballing entertainment, with 32 nations battling it out for the right to be crowned world champions. But who are the men who will be carrying the hopes and expectations of their respective countries?

Find out with **FIFA World Cup Superstars**, a photo celebration of the most talented players in the world who will be certain to thrill us all this soccer summer:

Carlos Valderrama, Gabriel Batistuta, Dennis Bergkamp, Jorge Campos, John Collins, Didier Deschamps, Marcel Desailly, Youri Djorkaef, Gheorghe Hagi, Viktor Ikpeba, Kasey Keller, Jürgen Klinsmann, Frank de Boer, Brian Laudrup, Paolo Maldini, Ariel Ortega, Raúl, Romario, Ronaldo, Matthias Sammer, Peter Schmeichel, David Seaman, Alan Shearer, Hristo Stoichkov, Davor Suker, Ivan Zamoramo, Zinedine Zidane, Gianfranco Zola and Andoni Zubizarreta.

With pen portraits and career fact files, no football fan will want to be without this book as the World Cup circus pitches up in France.

CARLTON

ISBN 1-85868-441-2

£3.99

Picture Credits: *Left to right* Alan Shearer (Sporting Pictures (UK) Ltd.); Marcel Desailly (Empics/Tony Marshall); Ronaldo (Allsport UK Ltd./Shaun Botterill).

B

OFFICIAL LICENSED PRODUCT

FIFA WORLDCUP Guide for KIDS

©1995 ISL TM

SIXTY-FOUR FOOTBALL MATCHES; 96 hours of play — not to mention time added on for injuries and stoppages, extra-time and penalty shoot-outs; only six rest days from 10 June to 12 July; the best players in the world; the most modern stadiums; warm summer sunshine. World Cup France 98 ... Wicked entertainment!

FEATURES:
- Descriptions of all the stadiums in which the matches will take place.
- Do-it-yourself results table that allows you to chart the progress of the successful teams from the initial group matches through the all-important knock-out stages of the tournament.
- An easy-to-follow guide to how all the nations made it through the testing qualifying rounds.
- 60 full-colour action photographs and colour artworks of the team strips and national flags of all 32 participants.

The World Cup has arrived.
Be a part of it with

The FIFA World Cup Guide for Kids

ISBN 1-85868-443-9

9 781858 684437

£3.99

Picture Credits: *Left to right* · Roberto Carlos (Allsport UK Ltd./Vandystadt/Frederic Nebinger); Alan Shearer (Empics/Matthew Ashton); Paolo Maldini (Allsport UK Ltd./Ben Radford).

TAPE

Type
What type of text am I constructing? What codes can I use?

Audience
Who is it aimed at? Age? Gender? Interests?

Purpose
What is it trying to do? How shall I try to do this? (How do I want the audience to feel? How can I use signs to get this response?)

Effectiveness
Will it work? (Show a friend, check it out and change bits if necessary.)

Construction task 1:

Publicity for a 'Safe Rave'

A 'Safe Rave' is going to be held in your town, to raise funds for helping refugees. The event is for 13–16 year olds. The police are in favour of this event and will be around to ensure people's safety. Publicity must stress that it is a drug-free, alcohol-free event. The event will feature a laser light show, prizes for wacky outfits, and live bands.

Draft the text for two single-sided leaflets. The purpose of both is to inform readers about the event, and to make it sound exciting and attractive.

Leaflet one: The audience is young people aged 13–16.

Leaflet two: The audience is the teachers at all the local secondary schools. Its purpose is to get them to encourage students to attend the event.

Think carefully about the construction of each leaflet, and the presentational devices you might use. Use language signs to suit your audience and purpose. Ask yourself the questions on the left to help you plan and assess your leaflet.

Write some notes to say how you have used language signs to inform and persuade your audience.

Deconstruction task 2

Here is a pair of reports on the same event: one each from a broadsheet and a tabloid.

A

Tot saved by mum

By MAXINE FRITH

BRAVE mum Jill Bettelley has saved the life of her dying baby by donating part of her liver.

Her 18-month-old son Luke had just 48 hours to live after he was diagnosed with acute liver failure.

There was no suitable liver donor available. The only option was a pioneering transplant.

Jill, 32, said: 'I could have died on the operating table, but that didn't even come into it. My only concern was Luke.'

She is now recovering at home in Worthing, West Sussex, after surgery at London's King's College Hospital.

Its spokesman said: 'Luke's stable and improving. We are optimistic he'll make a full recovery.'

The operation on March 5 was the first time in the UK that a transplant from a living-relative donor had been performed on a patient whose liver had ceased functioning.

B

Mother saves her baby's life

A MOTHER saved the life of her dying baby by donating part of her liver for a transplant operation that has made British medical history, it emerged yesterday.

Eighteen-month-old Luke Bettelley was given 48 hours to live after he was taken to hospital with acute liver failure and no suitable donor could be found. However, doctors at King's College Hospital, London, were able to transplant part of the liver from his mother, Jill, in a pioneering operation that could save more lives.

The procedure has been performed three times in the US and once in Germany. Both mother and baby are now recovering after undergoing the operation on March 5.

1 Denotation

(noting what is there)

a Read the two reports carefully and note down what they are about by using the five Ws questions.

b Note down any obvious uses of language signs. Can you find slang or adjective tags in either text? Does either text use the passive voice a lot?

c Compare the facts given by each report. Are the facts the same or different?

2 Connotation

(meaning and effects)

a Decide which is the tabloid report and which is the broadsheet report. Explain how you decided – talk about the content of the reports and the language signs they use.

b Which report helps you to understand most about the event? Why is this? Are more facts given? Is it explained more clearly?

c Explain whether or not the language signs in the reports play on your emotions.

d Is either of the reports biased in any way? If so, say in what ways it is biased.

Construction task 2

Newspaper writers get information about events from a range of sources. These may include news agencies, on-the-spot reporters, eye-witnesses, and the emergency services. The writer then has to construct the article by selecting from these various sources. What they select affects the style of the article – and this depends on the newspaper's readership as well as its editorial policy.

Here are your news sources.

News agency source:

Airliner on flight from London to Miami crashed off Florida coast. Many deaths suspected but not confirmed. Suspected casualties include teenage film idol Raphael Gabrini recently nominated for Oscar in blockbuster movie 'The Trekker'. Casualties taken to Dade County Hospital Miami. Reports of many bodies in water. Crowds of anxious film fans at hospital gates. Rumour of bomb being cause.

Police chief Alex Garner:

'Early reports suggest another aircraft may have been involved. Wreckage was scattered over a wide area. There are quite a lot of survivors as the pilot managed to make a belly land on the water. The pilot, Gus Stevens, was a hero. Local boats went out to help in the rescue which was only a mile off shore. Those guys really saved some lives.'

This page and page 60 show information about a fictional event from a range of sources.

In a group, write two articles each based on this information:

1 an article for a tabloid newspaper like the *Mirror* or *Sun*.

2 an article for a broadsheet newspaper like the *Times* or *Telegraph*.

Each article should have an appropriate headline and sub-headings and should be set out in columns. Indicate the kind of illustrations (photographs, sketches or diagrams) and captions which would accompany the written text.

The styles of writing which you use should be significantly different.

1 **The tabloid article.** This is likely to use language signs such as emotive language, slang, and a dramatic, eye-catching headline which may use a pun or alliteration. The syntax is likely to create a fast, slick rhythm and use the active voice. The article is likely to express strong opinions.

2 **The broadsheet article.** This is likely to use less emotive language and use the passive voice more often. The syntax is likely to create a slower, more controlled rhythm. The article is likely to rely more on facts than opinions.

Local boat owner Charlie Gonzales:

'We heard the plane's engines from the harbor. It was scary. Then there was a small explosion and the plane just dived. Then the nose came up and she hit the water. We got in our boats and made straight for the scene. There was mess everywhere. Screams, sirens, people in the water. We picked up this young blonde guy. Someone said he was a film star. He wasn't breathing well so I gave him mouth to mouth. He looked kinda blue. Then the medical guys took him away.'

Teenage film fan Gina Stephens:

'We've been waiting all night to know whether it's true. It's like a living nightmare, real agony, not knowing whether Raphael's alive or dead. It's like in a movie. I can't believe this is really happening. They say he may be brain damaged. It's all so terrible.'

Hospital porter George Hennessey:

'I've never seen scenes like this. There must be thousands of youngsters here. They're in a real state – fainting, weeping over this film guy. I did see his movie last week. He's a real good actor. Let's hope the doctors can pull him through this. It feels just like when Elvis died. People couldn't believe it.'

Hospital bulletin:

90 confirmed fatalities. 100 injured. Raphael Gabrini on life-support system. He has severe internal bleeding and head injuries. May have been saved by first aid of boat rescuer.

Ask yourself these questions to help you plan and assess your articles:

Type
What type of text am I constructing? What codes can I use?

Audience
Who is it aimed at? Age? Gender? Interests?

Purpose
What is it trying to do? How shall I try to do this?
(How do I want the audience to feel? How can I use signs to get this response?)

Effectiveness
Will it work? (Show a friend, check it out and change bits if necessary.)

Written language and still graphic images

The knowledge you already have

So far we have examined separately the codes of written language and still graphic images. In media texts, these codes are usually combined – this unit looks at texts which use both codes.

Checklist of graphic signs

Figure signs
  Face signs
  Hand signs
  Body signs
Shape, proportion
Colour, texture, lighting
Viewpoint

Checklist of language signs

Alliteration
Assonance
Adjective tag
Rhyme
Slang
Emotive language
Puns
Syntax/rhythm
Imagery
Active/passive voice
Imperative verbs
Interrogative verbs
Presentational devices

▽

When you deconstruct the texts, don't forget to use **two-step reading**:

1 Note the use of language and graphic signs and describe them (denotation).

2 Say what the signs mean and what effect they might have on their audience (connotation).

Sum up each text with the TAPE model – ask yourself:

Type
What sort of text is this? What codes does it employ?

Audience
Who is the audience? (Age? Gender? Interests?)

Purpose
What is the text trying to do? What is it trying to make its audience think and feel, in order to do this?

Effectiveness
Do you think the text would achieve its purpose?

▽

When you are constructing texts, ask yourself these questions:

Type
What type of text am I constructing?
What codes can I use?

Audience
Who is it aimed at? Age? Gender? Interests?

Purpose
What is it trying to do? How shall I try to do this? (How do I want the audience to feel? How can I use signs to get this response?)

Effectiveness
Will it work? (Show a friend, check it out and change bits if necessary.)

Task zone

Deconstruction task 1: The graphic novel – Buffy the Vampire Slayer

First read the page and make sure you understand the sequence of events. Now work through the questions to deconstruct the text.

1 **Denotation** (noting what is there): starting with the first frame, study each frame carefully and make notes to answer the questions.

a Look at the overall composition – what is in the foreground and the background? Are there any strong diagonal lines? Is it a close-up or a long shot? Is the viewpoint from high up, low down or eye level?

b Now make notes on figure signs: facial expressions, hand and body gestures. What is the colour and style of hair and clothing?

c Make notes on setting, the use of colour, light and texture.

d Does the action seem to come out of any frame?

e Now look at the language signs. Is the shape and style of lettering the same in all frames?

f Can you spot any uses of slang?

2 **Connotation** (meanings and effects): using your notes, write detailed answers to these questions.

a What effect is created by the colours used for the vampires' clothing and eyes?

b How is the viewpoint in frame 2 different from frame 3? How does this affect our impression of Angel in frame 2 and Buffy in frame 3?

c What does Angel's changing expression between frames 2 and 4 signal about how he is feeling in these two frames?

d Look again at the frames where objects break out of the box. What effect does this have on the way the action is portrayed?

e Compare the use of colour and strong diagonal lines in frames 1, 3 and 4 with the composition of frame 5. How is the atmosphere of frames 1, 3 and 4 different from that of frame 5?

f Look at what Buffy and Angel say in frames 1–4 and frame 5. How does the change in syntax/rhythm alter the mood in frame 5?

g Sum up what you think about this text by answering the TAPE key questions (see page 61).

Construction task 1: Creating a character/story-line for a new graphic novel (group task)

2 4 5 Imagine that you are trying to interest a publisher of graphic novels in a new idea for a fictional character aimed at a young teenage audience.

1 **Character profile:** Write down details about your character: age, physical features, personality, background, talents, weaknesses, likes, dislikes, best friends and enemies.

2 **Graphic image:** If possible, include sketches of your character and other characters in the story. Alternatively give detailed notes which a graphic artist could use in drawing your characters.

3 **Story outline:** Give a brief plot summary for the first story your character will be involved in.

4 **Opening frames:** Roughly sketch the opening four frames of your graphic novel giving notes on the graphic signs you would want to use. Try in your notes to say why these signs should be used.

Deconstruction task 2: the magazine holiday advert

This advert is constructed using photo-montage: a combination of a number of photos. You will need to look at the content of all the photos to describe the overall effect of the text.

▽

1 **Denotation** (noting what is there): starting at the top of the frame, work down, making notes on what you can see.

a What are the surroundings of the hotel like? Describe the design of the hotel.

b What are the people doing? Describe their appearance and gestures.

c What viewpoints are used in each image? Do we see scenes from high up, low down, from close up or at a distance?

d Now look at the language signs. Write down any emotive words you can find.

e Look at the length and structure of sentences (syntax). Are the sentences simple or complicated to read? Is the rhythm slick and fast or calm and gentle?

f Find one example each of assonance and alliteration, and two of imagery.

2 **Connotation** (meanings and effects): now, using your notes, explain in more detail.

a What impression is the advert trying to give of the type of holiday which is on offer at Sandals? Think about both language signs and graphic signs.

b Look at all the figure signs. What are we meant to think about the feelings of the people at this hotel?

c What atmosphere are the use of colour and lighting trying to create?

d Sum up what you think about this text by answering the TAPE key questions (see page 61).

Construction task 2: Magazine advertisement

▽

2 A new energy drink for young people doing sports is to be launched.

4 **5** You must design a full-page magazine advert, suitable for a popular teenage magazine.

First, think of a name for the drink. Ask yourself the TAPE construction questions (see page 61) to help you plan your advert.

Then sketch your advert design. Use notes and arrows to show how you will use graphic signs, like colour, viewpoint, shading, and figure signs.

Decide what language signs you will use. Can you create a catchy rhyme, or a slogan using alliteration and/or emotive words?

Lastly, use the TAPE questions again to make notes summing up what you have done and why you think it might be effective.

Feel the Magic of the Caribbean

Sandals' Halycon St. Lucia is a rare gem on a brilliant emerald sea. This enchanted paradise is designed with a rainbow of colour as rich as the island's culture. You will be mesmerized by the Caribbean magic of this unique resort, where excitement and tranquillity coexist in perfect harmony. And a casual elegance prevails within a world created for romance and pleasure. Couples can experience a host of land and water sports such as water skiing, snorkelling and scuba diving as well as true beachfront rooms and three gourmet restaurants including the unique Pierhouse restaurant, perhaps the Caribbean's most impressive dining experience. Best of all, you can indulge in all the pleasures of Sandals St. Lucia including golf, dining and entertainment as part of our "Stay At One, Play At Two" programme. Perfect for a holiday or a honeymoon… perfect for a man and a woman in love. For more information contact your travel agent or call 0800 742 742.

Sandals® HALCYON ST. LUCIA

Deconstruction tasks 3: The leaflet – Look After Your Heart

LOOK AFTER Y♥UR HEART

Every organ of your body needs a constant supply of blood to deliver the oxygen you need to survive. Guess who's poor job that is? Imagine having to work 24 hours a day, 7 days a week for your entire life without ever taking a break. It makes you realise why you have to take care of your heart. Especially when you discover heart disease can start early in life.

Oh sure it's hard to think about the future, but how you treat your heart now has a big difference on how it will treat you later on. Right now cardiovascular disease (CVD - diseases of the heart and blood vessels) is the main cause of death in the UK. Every 2 minutes there's someone having a heart attack. In fact, it's the cause of almost one in every two deaths. Ouch! But it doesn't have to be. Death rates from coronary heart disease (CHD - disease of coronary arteries) started to fall in the seventies and to make doubly sure that continues here's **4 WAYS TO KEEP YOUR HEART HEALTHY**

1 EAT WELL: What you eat has a direct effect on your heart so try to eat less fatty foods that block the arteries and stress out your heart. Try to eat more poultry, fish, fresh fruit, vegetables, lean meat, breads and cereals.

2 DON'T SMOKE: It's the single best thing you can do. Or, not do in this case.

3 PHYSICAL ACTIVITY: And we don't just mean go to the gym. Any activity that gets the heart pumping is great.

4 WATCH YOUR WEIGHT: The more weight you carry around the harder your heart has to work.

The way to a healthy heart is through the stomach

EAT LESS

EAT MORE

MEAT

FISH - CHICKEN

BREADS - CEREALS

FRUIT - VEGETABLES
(5 portions a day)

THE FOOD PYRAMID

When we talk about healthy eating we don't mean going on some kooky "nothing but lettuce for a whole week" kind of deal. We just mean the way you eat in general. It's all about finding a balance.

You need to watch all those yummy foods you know are high in fat and get into the more natural ones. Fresh fruits, veggies, even fish and chicken are perfect. That's not to say you can't indulge, it's just that you can't live, literally, on biscuits and sweets.

It's a bummer but that's life. So as you start keeping an eye on what you eat try this little quiz on your parents. It's a blast. Next time they're unpacking the shopping read some of the labels and start casually asking questions like:"What percentage of saturated fat is in that margarine?"

"How many calories in that pie comes from fat?"
"Is that milk skimmed or semi-skimmed?"
Then you quiz them on the recommended daily intakes for the most important nutrients listed on food labels.

MEN		WOMEN
95.0g	FAT	70.0g
2.5g	SODIUM	2.0g
70.0g	SUGAR	50.0g
20.0g	FIBRE	16.0g

Construction task 3: leaflet on the environment

1 **Denotation** (noting what is there)

a First read through the written part of the text. You'll soon notice that it is written in quite a chatty or colloquial style, using a number of slang words or phrases. Write down six examples of slang.

b Write down six facts and three opinions from the text.

c One of the things which makes the writing chatty is the syntax. Many sentences are quite short. Write down three of the shortest sentences.

d Leaflets which give advice often use imperative verbs (the command form, e.g. Sit down). Find four examples of the use of imperative verbs.

e Write down the use of alliteration in one of the sub-headings.

f Now look at the use of graphic images. What do the four images in the middle of the page show?

g Note where different fonts been used.

h Note where different colours have been used.

2 **Connotation** (meanings and effects)

a Who is the audience for this leaflet? How did you decide on your answer?

b What effect is the leaflet meant to have on the audience's thoughts and feelings? Mention how language and graphic signs have been used.

c What is your opinion of the construction of this leaflet? Will it be effective? Give reasons for your answer.

 Your task is to construct a leaflet about caring for the environment, with a particular focus on recycling. Your audience is young people aged 11–15.

Ask yourself the TAPE construction questions on page 61 to help you plan your leaflet.

Try to think of a good title for your leaflet. What style of text will you use?

What pictures will you use: what would the key images be?

On a large piece of paper, sketch the design of your leaflet. Use notes and arrows to show how you will use graphic signs and pictures.

Decide what language signs you will use – bear in mind your audience and the purpose of your leaflet. Will you use slang, emotive language, alliteration, rhyme?

Lastly, use the TAPE questions again to make notes summing up what you have done and why you think it might be effective.

Deconstruction task 4: the internet website – The York Dungeon

1 **Denotation** (noting what is there)

a What colours are used and where?

b Next look at the images: look at the use of objects, figures, viewpoint, shapes, lighting and shading.

c Look at the shape of the icons which take you to other pages of the website.

d Now look at the language signs. Note down three uses of emotive words.

e Look at the style of print – the font shapes, words which are written in bold type.

f Note any uses of imperative verbs and interrogative verbs.

g Find two examples of the use of alliteration.

2 **Connotation** (meanings and effects)

a What kind of atmosphere have the colours been chosen to create?

b Why have the images included been chosen?

c What effects are created by the use of lighting and viewpoint?

d Give examples of language being used to create atmosphere and make the York Dungeon sound worth visiting.

e How have text fonts been used for effect? Comment particularly on the way the 'the York Dungeon' is written.

f Sum up what you think about this text by answering the TAPE key questions (see page 61).

Construction task 4: your own website

Even if you haven't got internet access yet, you can plan what your website would contain. If you already have a website, design an extra page, or see if you can improve on your current page. You can either create just a home page or a series of pages.

Remember your audience could be global! What messages about yourself will you send out? Taste in music? Details of the family? Your home and neighbourhood? Favourite sports team? Hobbies?

What images will you include? What text styles will you use? What kind of language signs will work well to give an impression of your personality? Ask yourself the TAPE construction questions on page 61 to help you plan your website.

Using a sheet of plain paper for each page of the website, sketch the layout and indicate the contents of each page with notes. Compose the written text separately and then insert it on to your pages.

Lastly, use the TAPE questions again to make notes summing up what you have done and why you think it might be effective.

the York Dungeon

A perfectly horrible experience.

Deep in the heart of historic York, buried beneath its very paving stones,
lies the North's most chillingly famous museum of horror.
The York Dungeon brings more than 2,000 years of gruesomely
authentic history vividly back to life and death.
As you delve into the darkest chapters of our grim and bloody past, recreated in all its dreadful detail,
remember, everything you experience really happened.
A warning – in the Dungeon's dark catacombs it always pays to keep your wits about you.
The 'exhibits' have an unnerving habit of coming back to life…

Don't be afraid to scream. You won't be alone.

At the York Dungeon you can step back in time and learn about the darker side of European history.
You can unravel the truth about York's turbulent and colourful past.
Catch the Plague – the Black Death which wiped out
one-third of Europe's population.
Follow the notorious highwayman Dick Turpin on his
journey to the gallows.
Confront the ghostly Lost Roman Legion.
And see the rise and fall of one of York's most notorious sons – Guy Fawkes,
the villain of the Gunpowder Plot.

Dare you enter the Dungeon?

The Plague   Dick Turpin   The Dungeon   Dungeon Secrets

Deconstruction task 5: newspaper extracts

These extracts are from two articles about Henri Paul, the driver of the car in which Princess Diana died. The questions about the articles are on page 72.

CRASH DRIVER   The Mirror   Wednesday, September 3, 1997

SPEED FREAK

Bike nut could down nine whiskies a night

SUPERBIKE: Powerful Yamaha motorcycle

HORROR: The wrecked Mercedes after the 121mph tunnel smash

by PETER ALLEN and TED OLIVER

DRUNKEN security boss Henri Paul popped out for a large whisky just an hour before he drove the car in which Princess Diana died.

He downed the nightcap in one go after already drinking the best part of two bottles of wine in his Paris apartment on Saturday night.

Speed-freak Paul, 41, a former air force pilot and motorbike fan, was a formidable boozer who could down nine whiskies in one night, it emerged last night.

He was more than three times over the limit when he smashed the high-powered Mercedes into a tunnel wall at 121mph, killing Diana, her new love Dodi Fayed and himself.

Colleagues, friends and drinking companions were left asking: 'How could a man like this have been allowed to get behind the wheel with the Princess of Wales in the back of his car?'

Party-loving Paul had spent his Saturday night off, knocking back wine as he watched TV.

At 11pm, he walked next door to the Le Bourgogne bar for a large glass of his favourite tipple.

Binges

Minutes later, he got the call from the Ritz Hotel, where he was deputy head of security.

He was told he was needed urgently to drive Diana and Dodi away from a hoard of waiting paparazzi at the hotel.

A source at the Ritz Hotel said Paul was 'over-excited and as drunk as a pig' when he arrived back for his last job.

He did not consider for a second turning down his bosses' plea for a driver.

Paul's drinking binges were not confined to the Ritz. He was a regular at numerous bars around the French capital.

At Willi's wine bar just up the street from his apartment, the English owner Mark Williamson said: 'He used to be in here nearly every night.

'I always thought he looked a bit like a well-pissed Groucho Marx.'

Speed-mad Paul also liked to prop up the bars in his home town Lorient, in Brittany.

The former air force captain loved to fly home in a hired private jet, then thunder off to meet his pals on a 1100cc super bike.

His friend Phillippe Proussaid: 'We last saw Henri in June and he was his typical self, standing at the bar buying drinks for his friends.

'When he was working in Paris he worked damn hard but when he came off duty he knew how to have a good time.

'He liked fast bikes, jets and a good night out with his mates.

'I've known him to drink nine whiskies in one sitting – he was that kind of bloke. But we loved him and so did everyone else around here.

'He will be missed by everyone.'

The Guardian, Wednesday September 3, 1997

Michael Cole, the Al Fayed spokesman, talks to the press

The lifestyle of the driver: Henri Paul was known to friends and colleagues as a quiet, self-effacing man who only drank occasionally, had never been seen drunk and lived for his passions of flying and sailing

Mystery of a quiet man

Owen Bowcott and Jon Henley in Paris

In the pavement cafés along the narrow Rue des Petits Champs where Henri Paul lived, none of the bar owners knew the dead driver as a habitual or heavy drinker. Lifelong friends in Brittany, where he was born and brought up, said they had never known him drunk.

Nor was there any clue yesterday to explain why the 41-year-old deputy head of security at the Ritz Hotel – described as a serious man and a cool-headed professional – should have driven a Mercedes S280 while more than three times over the French alcohol limit.

Bertrand, owner of the Royal Vendôme brasserie, round the corner from the Ritz in the Rue Danielle Casanova, recalled seeing Paul at around 7pm on Saturday, just after he had come off duty. 'He had a Perrier Hirondelle, without alcohol, and a whisky – a White Horse I think,' he said. 'He drank alone and was very quiet – he was just having one before going home.

'He would be in here perhaps once every three months. It was quite unusual to serve him. But I've never seen him drunk and I've been here seven years. He was very polite and self-effacing. Never exuberant.'

At some stage during the evening Paul was recalled to the Ritz, when the hotel's management decided it needed more drivers to divert the waiting photographers' atten-

The building in central Paris which was home to Henri Paul, the driver

tion away from Diana, Princess of Wales and Dodi Al Fayed. When and where he drank the rest of the alcohol remains a mystery.

A former air force captain, Paul divided his time between the Ritz, his native Britanny, and a small flat in a rundown block in the Rue des Petits Champs.

Marcel Douzier, from Port Louis, near Lorient, who had known Paul since his schooldays, said Paul was 'really a calm and sen-

sible type' who had kept up his pilot's licence by flying regularly, and was also a keen sailor.

'You don't keep a flying licence if you're a drunkard,' he said.

Jean-Louis Le Baraillac, an Air France pilot who trained Paul in the 1970s, said he was a fanatical flyer. 'He was a very nice guy, very serious. A good bloke,' Mr Baraillac said. 'And he took his work seriously. He was proud of his position at the Ritz.'

▽

1 **Denotation** (noting what is there): keep separate notes about each article.

a Look at the images used in each article – what does each one show?

b Now look at the headlines, sub-headings and captions. Make a note of any emotive words used. Can you spot the use of alliteration, assonance and slang?

c Read both articles a few times, then make a note of the facts about Henri Paul that each article gives you. Are the facts in the two articles the same or different?

d Next, try to find examples of opinions. These might include opinions of the articles' writers as well as the opinions of people quoted.

e Can you find the use of adjective tags, emotive words and slang? Which article uses these features the most?

2 **Connotation** (meanings and effects): now use your notes to back up your answers to these questions.

a Explain what impressions the *Guardian* article gives of Henri Paul. Refer to the use of language signs and images.

b What impression of Henri Paul does the *Mirror* article give? Refer to the use of language signs and images.

c What is the purpose of each article?

d What overall effect is each article intended to have on its audience?

e What effect does each article have on you? Which one do you believe? Give reasons for your answer.

Construction task 5: newspaper articles

▽

2
4
5

It's clear that the way Henri Paul is represented in the above articles is very different. The *Mirror* gives a strongly negative impression of Paul. The *Guardian* gives quite a positive impression.

Choose a fairy story or other traditional tale. Then write two articles:

1 a short article for a broadsheet newspaper which gives a negative impression of a character in the story.

2 a short article for a tabloid newspaper which gives a positive impression of the same character.

For example you could re-tell Little Red Riding Hood, suggesting in one version that the wolf was violent and evil. In the other version he could be a rather sad, lonely character – possibly even cruelly trapped by the little girl and her grandmother.

Ask yourself the TAPE construction questions on page 61 to help you plan your articles. Remember to use the appropriate broadsheet and tabloid styles (see pages 52–53 to remind yourself). Include headlines, captions, and sketches of the images which should go with the articles.

Lastly, use the TAPE questions again to make notes summing up what you have done and why you think it might be effective.

The code of sound

In this unit, you will be exploring the code of sound by examining how you read sounds and how sounds are used in sending media messages.

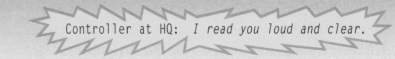

Police Officer on radio: *Approaching scene of accident. How do you read me?*

Controller at HQ: *I read you loud and clear.*

The knowledge you already have

You already know quite a lot about reading sounds. See how much by trying this sound quiz.

> **1** What sound is used to signal the end of a lesson in school?
>
> **2** What sound is used to signal a fire in school? (How is this different from your answer to question 1)?
>
> **3** What sounds does a concert audience use to signal approval?
>
> **4** What sounds might be used at a football match to signal disapproval?
>
> **5** What sound is used to signal the start of a running race?
>
> **6** What is a wolf whistle? How is it different from whistling to attract a friend's attention?
>
> **7** When you make a telephone call, what are the different sounds which signal the number is ringing and the number is engaged?

In your daily life you are bombarded by sound signs. You quickly learn to recognize their meanings.

Media texts in radio, television and film use a wide range of sound signs to create meanings for their audiences. Working out how sounds are used in media texts is about reading those sounds.

Learning zone

If you are going to crack the code of sound, you need to understand the difference between hearing and listening. They are similar but not the same. You may have a radio switched on at home and you will hear that it's on. However, you may not be listening to it – listening needs some concentration.

Hearing tends to be passive. Listening is much more active. Try these activities in pairs to test the difference.

▽

> 1 A and B sit opposite each other. Each chooses a topic to talk about for one minute. At the teacher's signal, both start talking at the same time about their topics. At the stop signal, A has to say what B was talking about and vice versa.
>
> 2 A and B take turns to play each part in this activity. A starts silently reading a page in a book. After a few seconds, with A still reading, B spends half a minute telling A what they did last night. Swap round and then compare what you heard.

These activities should show you that it's difficult to listen properly when you are thinking about or doing something else. To appreciate the ways in which sound is used in media texts, you will need to concentrate on listening – and know what to listen out for.

What makes up the code of sound?

The code of sound includes all the ways in which sounds are used to send messages. This includes music, speech, sound effects (SFX) and the use of silence.

We will be using two-step reading to decode sound texts, as we have with the other codes. But using two-step reading with the code of sound isn't always easy, as we tend to react to sounds immediately, as they happen. However, always try to keep two-step reading in mind when you're trying to decode the way sounds are being used – identify the sounds (denotation), and describe their effects (connotation).

Let's look at how to describe and understand the different components of sound.

Speaking voices

Probably the first thing you take note of when you hear an actor in a film or a DJ on the radio is what their voice is saying. But voices have other qualities which have an effect on you without your necessarily being aware of them. In this section we'll look into the various qualities which make up the speaking voice.

Volume

This refers to how loud or quiet a voice is. There are many different ways to describe slight differences in volume.

▼

1 With a partner, write a list of words which describe a voice when it's loud, e.g. bellowing.

2 Now write a list of words describing a voice when it's quiet, e.g. murmuring.

3 Name three situations when a loud voice might be used. Why would you use a loud voice in these situations?

4 Name three situations when a quiet voice might be used. Why would you use a quiet voice in these situations?

Pitch

This refers to how high or low a voice is. You can describe the pitch of a voice as high, medium or low.

▼

1 What voice pitch is likely to be used when expressing the following feelings?
   a surprise
   b sadness
   c terror
   d sympathy

2 Get a partner to listen to the way your voice changes in this activity.

   Try saying the following phrase as if you are feeling the emotions in a, b, c, and d above, changing the pitch of your voice as appropriate.

Oh no, I don't believe it.

   Can you describe the way your partner changed the pitch of their voice for each emotion?

Pace

This refers to the speed of the voice. As with volume, you can use a lot of different words to describe pace.

▼

1 Make a list of words you might use to describe the pace of someone's voice.

2 Say how fast you would expect someone to talk if they were feeling:

  a bored   **c** hysterical

  b excited   **d** contented.

Now try this next activity to see what effects you can get by combining pitch, pace and volume.

▼

1 With a partner, take turns to read out loud the following snippets of sports commentary. As you do so, change the pitch, pace and volume of your voice, to suit what you are saying.

Snooker:

'... And here we are in a packed Crucible Theatre joining these two young players for the semi-final of the world snooker championship. And it's the youngster from London to start. There's intense concentration on the faces of this audience...'

Motor-racing:

'... And it's Coulthard in a superb display of precision driving, overtaking Hakkinen and entering the fifteenth lap – he's lapped Schumacher and – oh no, he's clipped the bank and gone into a spin...'

Cricket:

'... And here comes the young Leicestershire left-hander; it's a well-pitched ball but it's driven hard. They'll take a single. But, no, they're going for a second. And it's a superb piece of fielding by Turner and it's going to be a run-out. Yes, a clear mistake by Scott who's run out for six.'

2 As you listen to your partner, make notes about how they are using pitch, pace and volume.

3 Now discuss what you did, and the different ways you and your partner combined volume, pitch and pace in the commentaries. Decide whose commentary used the most convincing combination.

Rhythm

The rhythm of your voice refers to the way you place emphasis on certain words. Changing the rhythm can affect the meaning of what you are saying.

▼

Read the sentence given, placing emphasis only on the words in bold. You could do this with a partner, taking turns to speak and listen.

a Will you go and find her now?

b Will you go and **find** her now?

c Will you **go** and **find** her **now**?

d Will you go and find **her** now?

e Will **you** go and find her now?

Which of the versions sounded: very bossy? like pleading/begging?

Word sounds and rhythm

In some media texts, words will be very carefully chosen for their sounds and the rhythms they create when spoken. (Remind yourself of what you learnt in unit 3 (pages 40–44) about the way word sounds are used in slogans and other texts.) Listen out for language signs such as emotive words, alliteration, assonance, and rhyme in creating the rhythm of a slogan or jingle.

▼

1 Look back at the holiday brochure texts on page 44 ('Go Greek' and 'Make Mine Ibiza').

   a How do the words used affect the rhythm of the text?

   b Now imagine these as radio adverts. How will you read them? How will you use your voice to create the right mood? Try them out and let your partner be the judge!

2 Look at these slogans.

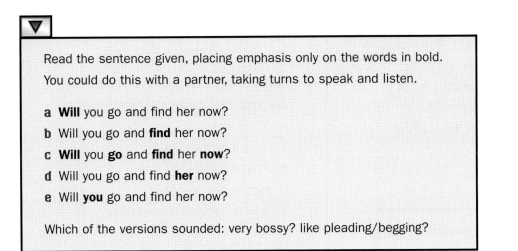

You can't get better than a **Kwik-Fit** Fitter.

A **Mars** a day helps you work rest and play.

In both, the rhythm is created by the clever use of assonance and alliteration. The first slogan's short vowel sounds and hard consonants give a clipped and lively rhythm. In the second, longer vowel sounds and softer consonants create a more flowing, leisurely rhythm.

Why have the advertisers used these different rhythms? What connotations do the rhythms have for what is being advertised?

Tone

Tone is another important aspect of sound. It refers to the feeling you get from a sound. This comes from a combination of the volume, pitch, pace and rhythm, as well as the situation in which the sound is being used. The tone of someone's voice could be soothing and gentle, or it could be harsh, threatening, or sinister. Actors will use a particular tone of voice to convey a mood or feeling.

Look at this grid. One column contains different situations, and the other contains possible tones of voice. Fit one tone of voice to each situation.

Situation	Tone of voice
a Salesperson trying to sell a product	1 Playful
b Bully picking on a younger child	2 Sympathetic
c Friends having a laugh	3 Superior
d Grandparent calming down a crying child	4 Aggressive
e Older sister bossing her younger sister	5 Persuasive

Tone is one of the key signs which creates meaning. For example, a loud, high-pitched voice could be expressing terror (someone screaming), or happiness (a child yelling for joy). It is the tone of that voice which will make the difference in what you understand from it.

1 Using the line of conversation below, take turns with a partner to practise changing the tone of your voice. Each time your partner says the line, make a note of the way they are using volume, pitch, pace and rhythm to change their tone.

Say 'Oh, hello. I've been hoping to meet you for such a long time. Heard such a lot about you':

a using a caring tone

b using a threatening tone

c using a playful tone

d using a hurried/offhand tone.

2 Working in pairs again, try expressing the dialogue below in three different ways by varying your voice signs. Take it in turns to be A and B.

a A: angry teacher, B: troublesome pupil

b A: grandparent, B: grandchild

c A: employer, B: employee

Vary the volume, pace, pitch, tone and rhythm. Place emphasis on different words as appropriate.

A: Come over here. I want to speak to you. And it's serious.

B: I'm very busy. Can it wait?

A: No. I don't think it can.

B: But I am in the middle of something.

A: I need you here now.

B: But...

A: No 'buts'.

B: Okay then.

Practise your three versions together, and then present them to another pair in the class.

Accent

A person's accent can be used as a powerful sign in a film or an advert. Actors in films or adverts often use a particular accent because the accent signals certain connotations.

RP (Received Pronunciation) accent

This accent is based on educated speech in southern England. It is used by many TV newsreaders, although some do have slight regional accents.

Regional and foreign accents

These are accents associated with a particular region or country, e.g. London (Cockney), Australian, Texan, Jamaican.

Accents have different connotations for people. People may judge accents positively or negatively, as you can see from this extract from a *Daily Mirror* report. It is about Jamie Shea, the man who was NATO spokesperson during the war in Yugoslavia in 1999.

Accent:

the way words and sentences are pronounced

▽

Read the list below. For each item, think of an example where a particular accent is used. Write down the name of the programme or product and try to describe the accent.

a Food advert
b News programme
c TV soap drama
d Comedy programme
e Car advert

Why Nato's canny Cockney kid is now worth megadosh

...Thousands of journalists hang on every word uttered by the chief NATO mouthpiece. ...

Not everyone has been impressed by his barrow-boy vowels. The wife of a Nato general was so offended that she sent a formal complaint to the Alliance HQ in Brussels.

A Nato official explains: 'Jamie's from London and is a real Cockney. That's how he talks and he doesn't care what other people think. No one here does.

'The UK military delegation received a formal complaint demanding why a man with such an accent was in such a position.

'Everyone just laughed.'

▽

Why do you think the general's wife was offended? What connotations might a Cockney accent have for her? Why did the military delegation laugh at the complaint?

An accent used in a radio or TV drama or comedy series can affect the way we react to a character – whether we think the character is weak, admirable, confident, aggressive, friendly, trustworthy, fun-loving, and how we judge their social standing. The media can reinforce both positive and negative connotations about an accent.

Dialect

People often confuse the words 'dialect' and 'accent'. **Accent** is the way words and sentences are pronounced. **Dialect** refers to the form of words used by people. A dialect may have its own special grammar rules, as well as its own words and expressions.

Standard English dialect

This was once a regional dialect but it is now used throughout the English-speaking world. It is no longer associated with any particular region. It is the dialect which is generally used in writing newspaper reports, textbooks, novels, and information leaflets. In speech, it is used in formal situations like interviews and news programmes.

Regional dialect

A regional dialect is usually related to a particular part of a country or area of the world. In media terms, regional dialects are most noticeable because they have different words or expressions from Standard English.

Here are some examples of regional dialect words/phrases and their Standard English equivalents:

Regional dialect	Standard English
to put the mockers on (Cockney)	to spoil or mess up
brucksy (Jamaican)	broken down
yhem (Geordie)	home
snap (South Yorkshire)	packed lunch
biggety (southern US)	conceited

Dialect words are often used in media texts to reinforce the impression given by an accent. For example, this Allinson bread slogan uses the Yorkshire dialect word 'nowt', meaning 'nothing':

Bread wi' nowt taken out

▼

1 Why do you think the makers of this advert chose to use the Yorkshire dialect word? What connotations about Allinson Bread were they hoping to generate?

2 In the grid below is a list of products. If you were creating an advert for each of them, which accent/dialect would you use? Copy the grid and write in your decisions, including what effect you hope this choice of accent/dialect would have on your audience. Think carefully about your audience, and how you will use accent or dialect to achieve your purpose.

Product	My choice of accent/dialect	The intended effect on the audience
pizza		
sports car		
fruit drink		
computer 'action' game		
cider		

Reading radio voices

Radio presenters are very skilful at using their voices to suit a particular kind of programme and audience. They know that an audience for classical music will expect a different style of presentation from a rock music audience.

▼

Listen to snippets of speech from a variety of radio channels: move the dial and listen to the voices as they come and go. How do you read which channel or programme each voice belongs to? Ask yourself these questions about each voice:

a What sort of channel do you think the voice belongs to?

b Is it high-pitched, medium or low-pitched?

c Is the voice speaking quickly or slowly?

d Is it loud or fairly quiet?

e Is the tone bouncy and excited, or serious and calm?

f What kind of accent is used?

g Which audience is the style of voice aimed at?

You could probably identify the different sorts of station quite easily from the voices you heard in the last activity. Now have a go at radio presentation.

Checklist of voice signs
Volume
Pitch
Pace
Rhythm
Tone
Word sounds
Accent, dialect

▽

Below is the start of a script which opens a radio programme. You are to read it for two different programmes. First decide what style of voice would be appropriate for each audience. Then try reading it, varying the sound signs as appropriate. Take turns with a partner and give each other feedback.

a Read it in the style of a presenter for a rock music programme.

b Read it in the style of a presenter for a classical music programme.

When you're happy with your presentations, record them on tape and/or present them to the rest of the class.

Good morning, and welcome to the programme.
We have a great selection of music for you this morning, plus readers' letters and a live interview with someone heading for the big time.

We'll be playing a selection of new releases and, of course, tracks from the CD which is topping the charts this week.

So let's not waste any more time.

You're tuned to 60 minutes of the best music on radio.
And that's a fact.

Sound effects (SFX)

These are sounds used in radio or screen drama to represent certain things, such as tyres screeching, rain falling, doors banging, animal noises, 'canned' laughter. SFX are particularly important in radio drama. They give the audience clues about what's going on, helping them to visualize the scene.

To be able to think about sound effects, you need to listen closely to sounds.

TICK TOCK

SPLAT!

Spend a few minutes with your eyes closed, listening carefully to the sounds around you. Think about these questions as you listen.

What sounds can you hear? Are they close or far away?

Then try to describe them to yourself. Are they clear or muffled? High or low in pitch? Loud or soft? Are they rhythmic?

When you have finished listening, make notes on what you heard. Then compare your findings with a partner's.

When sound effects are used in the media, a sound engineer has to think carefully about how to represent certain events. Creating the right combination of SFX can make a scene completely convincing – and getting it wrong can make things sound very silly.

Imagine you're a sound engineer for a radio drama. Discuss and make notes on the sounds involved in the following scenes:

a a person getting out of a car and going into their house.

b a child going into a shed and feeding a pet rabbit.

Apart from working out the sequence of sounds to make a scene believable, there is also the question of using sounds to create the right atmosphere (connotations). Sound effects are often used, especially in films and TV, to affect the mood of the audience.

Imagine you have to put together sound effects for a number of scenes in a radio drama.

Copy out this grid. One column gives you the scenes. In the other column, you must put in the SFX you would use to set the scene.

Scene	My choice of SFX
A pleasant summer afternoon in the country	
A miserable winter evening in the city	
A person entering a busy supermarket	
A person entering a haunted house	

Silence

Silence can be a very effective sound sign. When there is no sound at all, an audience is very aware of this. It is especially used in radio drama and in film soundtracks to create an atmosphere of suspense. The absence of other sounds unsettles an audience and makes them wonder what is about to happen.

Music

Music is used in the media for a range of different purposes. It is used to tell an audience that something is starting or ending, for example. Very often, it is used to influence an audience's thoughts and feelings – and it is extremely effective for this. When you're watching a film or a TV programme, you might not notice the way the music is affecting you – but music can be used to make us feel sad, happy, tense, frightened or excited.

Most of the sound signs you've learnt about in relation to speaking voices also relate to music (volume, pitch, pace, rhythm, and tone).

Write down where in the media where you might hear music:

a to make you feel sad

b to make you pay attention

c to make you laugh

d to signal to you that a programme has finished.

The most common use of music in media texts is in a soundtrack – a combination of sounds which go with a screen image. The soundtrack is often a mixture of music, speaking voices and sound effects.

Instrumental soundtracks

An instrumental soundtrack is made up of instrument sounds, rather than singing voices. When you hear an instrumental soundtrack, listen out for the instrument sounds being used in the music. Are they violins, cellos, electric guitars, acoustic guitars, harps, trumpets, saxophones, flutes, drums? Sometimes the instrument sounds will have been made by an orchestra, sometimes using a synthesizer. Either way, the instrument sounds will be chosen to create particular feelings in the audience.

▼

What sort of feelings or atmosphere might be created by using the following instrument sounds on a soundtrack?

a a loud electric guitar

b a harp

c fast drumming

d a flute

e loud trumpets

f a slow double-bass

Sometimes characters in films are even given their own 'signature tune' which is played whenever they appear. This is done in the film thriller *Jaws*, about a great white shark which terrorizes an American holiday resort. The shark's approach is always signalled by the sinister, gravelly sound of two notes played on a double-bass – starting slowly, then building up speed as the shark moves in for the kill!

Vocal (sung) soundtracks

A vocal soundtrack is one which uses a singer or chorus. When you hear a vocal soundtrack, note whether male or female voices are used. Ask yourself why a male or female has been chosen. How does this choice relate to the mood of the scene on the screen?

▼

Make a list of any films or TV programmes which have vocal soundtracks.

TV Programme Theme Tunes

The start and finish of every television programme are normally signalled by the use of music. Some long-running programmes have very well-known theme music.

The theme music will have been composed to suit the atmosphere and subject of the programme. So a comedy programme will probably have theme music which has a lively rhythm and a playful tone, while an emotional drama series will have a very different style of music.

Below is a sample of vocabulary which you may find useful when you're trying to describe sound signs. Use it for reference in the next activity.

Sound words box

Volume	thunderous, piercing, noisy, blaring, loud, hushed, quiet, low
Rhythm	calm, smooth, flowing, swinging, lively, broken, jerky, staccato, jarring, pulsating, emphatic, pounding
Pace	sluggish, drowsy, gentle, leisurely, quick, furious, slow
Pitch	high, medium, low
Tone (general)	dismal, sad, dreamy, pleasant, playful, aggressive, cutting, biting, sinister, comic
Tone of voice	bossy, sarcastic, unfriendly, witty, kindly, sympathetic, serious, enthusiastic

Choose two kinds of programmes from the list below. You are going to describe the opening music to one programme of each type you have chosen (referring to the sound words box for help describing the sound signs used).

a News

b Soap drama

c Sport programme

d Comedy programme

e Game show

First, record and listen to the music for each programme several times. Note down the way sound signs are used – types of instruments, rhythm, tone, pace, etc. (denotation). Then explain why this style of theme music has been used (connotation): what mood is it meant to signal to the audience?

You the 'composer'

Think about film soundtracks which you've heard. As you have seen, certain instrument sounds and SFX are used because of the mood and atmosphere they create. The way the two are combined can have a very powerful effect, and a lot of thought is given to this in creating soundtracks.

Checklist of sound signs

SFX
Silence
Speaking voices
Accent, dialect
Word sounds
Music
Instrument sounds

Volume
Pitch
Pace
Rhythm
Tone

▼

Copy out the grid below. The first column contains a number of scenes from TV and film drama. Imagine you are composing the soundtrack for these scenes.

Think carefully about each scene and the atmosphere you would want to create. Then choose a combination of instrument sounds, sound signs and sound effects which you think would have this effect. Use the lists on the right and the sound words box on page 86 to give you ideas.

Add this information to your grid, to build up a picture of the soundtrack. An example has been done for you.

Sound effects

Crickets chirping
Car tyres squealing
Footsteps on gravel
Breaking glass
Gun shots
Rain falling
Birds singing
Car horns
Waves breaking
Owl hooting
Car engine revving
Wind whistling
Police siren
Running footsteps
Creaking door

Instrument sounds

Spanish guitar
Violins
Electric guitar
Harp
Light drumming
Heavy drumming
Trumpets
Flutes
Steel band
Brass band
Cello
Double-bass

TV/Film scene	My choice of instrument sounds	My choice of other sound signs for the music	My choice of SFX
Family funeral	cello, flutes	quiet, low-pitched, gentle pace, sad tone, smooth rhythm	wind whistling, rain falling (both fairly quiet)
Gang fight on modern city street			
Romantic moonlit beach with teenage lovers			
Teenagers searching for vampire in churchyard at night			

Radio advertising

Radio adverts use all the sound signs you have met in this unit. Like all media texts, radio adverts have to be skilfully constructed, in order to convey a message. When constructing a radio advert, a writer will think carefully about their audience and purpose. Here are some tips from a radio advert writer, Steve Smith:

'... For many people, commercials are an annoying interruption. That means you have to do everything to make the commercials interesting – use striking sound effects, powerful music or funny situations and dialogue.

'Next it's vital to know WHO we're talking to, WHAT we want them to do and very importantly, WHY they should do it.

'Remember, radio commercials are typically only 30 or 40 seconds long. So don't put in too much information.

Repeat really important information, like the name of the advertiser, his address, phone number, or the offer if there is one, more than once...'

Types of radio advert

Adverts are designed for different purposes, and to appeal to different audiences.

a There is the straightforward persuasive type:
   'Go to X and buy Y.'

b There is the persuasive/informative type:
   'Don't miss the massive autumn sale which starts at 8am...'

c There is the advert with a storyline:
   'Morning Jim, where are you off to?'
   'I'm not missing that giveaway sale at X. Great bargains...'
   'Hey, wait on, I'll join you.'

Here is one of Steve Smith's scripts, which uses dialogue:

Key:
VO1 = Voice 1
VO2 = Voice 2
ANNC = Announcer

VO1: So we've done orange and pink walls, with carpet on the ceiling and bin liners for curtains. I think it looks great.

VO2: Well let's see what our couple think. Open your eyes… now!

(slight pause then joint, horrified scream, fading out)

ANNC: Luckily, there's one way to transform your home that everyone will love: just call in to Carlisle Glass! From a fresh coat of paint to completely new windows, we've everything you need to give your home and garden a stunning new look, with helpful staff to make sure you get the right advice. Visit us at Crown Street, Carlisle and see for yourself!

VO2: … so we painted him yellow and found a new home for his paintbrush. I think he looks great.

ANNC: Carlisle Glass. If only all transformations were as good!

1 First read the script a couple of times, then answer the questions:

   a What are the purposes of this advert? What is it trying to make its audience think and feel, in order to achieve these purposes?
   b Is it advertising a product or a service? What are the important details in the ad?
   c Who might be the audience for this advert? (Age? Gender? Interests?)
   d How does the advert try to grab the listener's attention?
   e What TV programme is this advert making fun of?
   f How does this advert attempt to persuade listeners?
   g Do you think it would work?

2 Now imagine you are a radio producer, and you can decide how the advert should actually sound.
   a What accents and tones of voice would you suggest for each of the three voices?
   b Rehearse the script, trying out different voices, accents, pitch, pace, etc. to see what styles of voice work best.
   c What SFX would you include in the advert?
   d Present your version of the advert to the class.

Task zone

Deconstruction task

Here is another advert by Steve Smith, written for
CFM, the Carlisle-based commercial radio station.
Read through the script, then answer the questions.

CLIENT: Go!Go!Go! Karting   **DUR:** 30"   **SCRIPT:** Steve

"MVO": Male Voice   "FVO": Female Voice   "SFX": Sound Effect

MVO 1: Manic, commentary style.   MVO 2: Very dynamic, powerful

---

(sfx race start)

MVO 1: ...AND IT'S GO! GO! GO!!

(Powerful, exciting music start)

MVO 2: You've watched Hill and Schumacher... now experience the incredible
excitement of motor racing for yourself at Go! Go! Go! Karting!
With full safety training and equipment provided it's ideal for
corporate entertainment, families, anyone over 8... and booking
isn't always necessary: just arrive and drive!

(sfx cars passing at speed)

Come and discover the most exciting leisure activity there is:
Go! Go! Go! Karting at Carlisle Airport! Call FREE on 0800 328
5293 for bookings or your free brochure!

MVO 1: It's GO! GO! GO! Karting!

Use two-step reading to look at the way Steve has constructed the script.

1 Denotation (noting what is there)

   a Identify the way sound signs are used. What SFX are used?

   b What style of voices are needed? (You'll need to find out what 'manic' means.) For each voice make notes on the pitch, pace, volume, tone, etc. which you think will be appropriate.

   c What kind of music is needed?

   d Look at the language signs. In the spoken text can you spot the use of: imperative verbs, emotive language, rhyme?

2 Connotation (meanings and effects)

   a Who is the audience for this advert?

   b What is the purpose of the advert? How have language signs and sound signs been used to achieve the purpose? What effect is the advert meant to have on the audience?

3 Sum up what you have found out about the advert with the TAPE key questions:

Type
What type of text is this? What codes does it use?

Audience
Who is the audience? (Age? Gender? Interests?)

Purpose
What is this text trying to do? What is it trying to make its audience think and feel, in order to do this?

Effectiveness
Do you think the text would achieve its purpose?

4 Now work with a partner on preparing a performance of this advert.

   a Read the script a couple of times to get a feel of the pace, tone, pitch, rhythm and volume which should be used.

   b Rehearse your version.

   c Then present your version to the rest of the class: either 'live' or as a recording.

Checklist of sound signs

SFX
Silence
Speaking voices
   Accent, dialect
    Word sounds
Music
   Instrument sounds

Volume
Pitch
Pace
Rhythm
Tone

Construction task: radio advert

4

6

You work for an advertising agency and you have to create a radio advert to promote one of the following:

a a new toothpaste

b an expensive perfume

c a new taxi company.

Before you start, plan what you will do, using the TAPE questions:

Type

What type of text am I constructing? What codes can I use?

Audience

Who is it aimed at? (Age? Gender? Interests?)

Purpose

What is it trying to do? How shall I try to do this?

(How do I want the audience to feel? How can I use signs to get this response?)

Effectiveness

Will it work? (Show a friend, check it out and change bits if necessary.)

1 Decide on a name for the product or company (remember alliteration and assonance can be useful).

2 Decide whether to compose a slogan.

3 Decide whether to compose a jingle – a rhyme sung to an appropriate rhythm and tune.

4 Write the spoken script which will be used in the advert. This could involve a scene with characters, or it could just be a persuasive description of the product or service (see *Types of radio advert*, page 88).

5 Decide on the music and/or SFX which will be used.

6 Write out the complete script.

7 Rehearse and then record the complete advert.

The code of moving images

Moving image texts include any type of communication which uses moving images. So they include cinema films, TV programmes, screen adverts, videos, computer games and animations.

In this unit you will come across some areas you've met before. For example, moving image texts generally have a soundtrack which can include music and voices. So this unit is dealing with a mixture of visual and sound codes, and the work you've done about the code of sound (unit 5, pages 73–92) will be useful here.

This unit will concentrate mostly on films, but you can apply what you learn here to any moving image text.

The knowledge you already have

You already have a wide experience of moving image texts. During your lifetime you will have watched hundreds of moving image sequences. Some may have been feature films at the cinema or on television. Others may have been screen adverts. All of these texts are constructed using the same range of signs.

We're going to start by reviewing what you know about films.

Genre films

There is a great variety of films but many films are of a particular type or **genre**. Examples of film genres are:

- western
- science fiction
- police/crime thriller
- historical drama
- horror
- romance

These genre films are made to a type of recipe or formula. It is a recipe which has been proved to work at the box office – so it is repeated to appeal to particular audiences.

▽

1 What audience would you say each of the genres listed on page 93 appeals to? Are they mainly young or old, male or female?

2 Make a list of as many films as you can think of which fit each genre, e.g. Science fiction – *Star Wars*. Then compare your list with a partner.

You recognize genre films because they have typical settings, characters, scenes, story-lines and props (props – short for 'properties' – include objects, gadgets, furniture, vehicles).

Let's take the Police/crime genre. What would you expect to find in this type of film?

Story-lines	Characters	Settings	Props	Clothing	Scenes
Murder	Mostly male	Cities	Cars	Suits – dark	Car chases
Kidnapping	Police	Offices	Guns	Uniforms	Shoot-outs
Robbery	Gangsters	Cheap hotels	Trucks	Expensive	Finding dead
Blackmail	Lawyers	Luxury	Expensive	clothes	bodies
Drug smuggling	News reporters	apartments	furnishings		Bank robberies

▽

7 Working with a partner, draw up a set of columns headed like the ones above. Then take each genre and list what you would expect to find in a typical film of that genre. Use your list of genre films to help you – what do the films you noted in each genre have in common?

Whatever genre a film belongs to, it is constructed using a common range of film signs. We're now going to look at the signs that a film-maker can use.

Learning zone

Constructing a film: telling a story in pictures and sound

What does a film-maker have to consider?

A film-maker generally starts with a story idea. This may be a new idea or it may be an adaptation of an existing story.

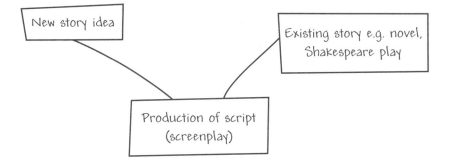

The screenplay

The screenplay is the script of the film. It is a writer's outline of what will be seen and heard on the screen. It tells the story of the film, but unlike a novel, it shows what the audience of the film will see and hear. Like a playscript, the screenplay will show the words spoken and the actions of the actors, but it will also include some details about camera shots, the soundtrack, and the location of the scenes.

The next two pages show an example of a screenplay, to show you how a scene from a novel might be adapted for the screen. It is taken from *The Silver Sword* – a story about a group of Polish children who get separated from their parents during the Second World War. In this scene, they are travelling in canoes to Switzerland. Ruth and Bronia are in one canoe. Edek and Jan are in the other. They discover Ludwig, the dog, is a stowaway on one canoe.

First read the scene from the novel, then look at how it has been turned into a screenplay.

Novel

They were in the grip of the current now, floating gently and steadily downstream. Edek and Jan were a length behind. She [Ruth] could hear the splash of their paddles in the water and Jan's voice calling. Had something gone wrong?

She backed water till they drew alongside.

'Don't shout, Jan,' she said.

'We're down at the bows. There's something very heavy inside, Ruth,' said Jan.

'Pass the stuff back to me. There's room astern,' said Edek.

Jan lifted the waist of his waterproof clear of the rim and reached underneath.

'Ow! It's wriggling – it's alive – and wet!' said Jan.

'Perhaps a fish has come up through the bottom,' said Bronia, much alarmed.

But Jan had guessed already what was hiding there. The wet thing was a nose. The stowaway was Ludwig.

Screenplay

Explanatory notes: EXT. = Exterior setting

EXT. CLOSE TO RIVER BANK. EVENING

1   The two canoes are a few metres apart drifting towards the main river current.
LONG SHOT following boats moving down river.
SOUND of water rushing.

2   CLOSE-UP of RUTH paddling. She looks anxious.

                    JAN (Out of view)
                      Hey!

At the sound of Jan's voice, RUTH glances over her shoulder.

                RUTH (In a 'stage whisper')
                Don't shout, Jan!

3   MEDIUM SHOT of Jan and Edek's canoe, from the front. Water is spilling in at the front of the canoe, and JAN looks worried.

                    JAN
We're down at the bows. There's something weighing us down at the front. It must be really heavy.

SOUND of water slapping side of canoe.
EDEK stops paddling and stretches out his hand to Jan.

> EDEK
> Pass the stuff back to me.
> There's room back here.

4 CLOSE-UP showing front of the canoe.
JAN leans forward pulling at waterproof. The edge of the canoe
dips under the water.
Rushing SOUND of river.

> JAN (In horror at what he feels under the waterproof)
> Ow! It's wriggling – it's alive – and wet!

5 CLOSE-UP of BRONIA'S face.
She looks scared.

> BRONIA
> Be careful – it could bite you.
> It might be a water snake or a rat!

6 MEDIUM SHOT of JAN, and the dog coming out from under the
waterproof. Jan's face breaks into a smile as he shakes his
head and pats the dog affectionately.

> JAN (Relieved)
> It's Ludwig!

Read the versions of the scene in the original novel and the adapted
screenplay. Then try to answer these questions.

1 Find an example in the screenplay of each of the following:
   a details of setting
   b type of camera shot
   c instructions that tell a character how to say a line
   d soundtrack details
   e instructions that tell a character what to do.

2 Compare the original extract with the screenplay. What differences in
dialogue can you find?

3 Divide an A4 sheet into six squares and see if you can sketch the shots
in this screenplay (they are numbered down the left-hand side).

Once the script is agreed on, the production of the film starts. Now the film-maker has to make a number of decisions:

1 What will be put in each scene? (This is called 'mise-en-scène', French for 'what is put into a scene', and includes casting, clothing, make-up, the way characters are positioned in a scene, props, sets and locations.)

2 How should the scene be lit? (This helps create the mood of a scene.)

3 What sort of camera shots will be used to shoot the scene? (What viewpoint should be used? Should the camera be moving with the action or standing still?)

4 How will the film sequence be edited? (This involves choosing which shots to use and how to link them – it creates the pace of the film.)

5 What should the audience hear (the soundtrack)?

Now we'll look at each of these five areas in turn.

Mise-en-scène

Setting

Where and when is the film to be set? In a city? In mountains or in a desert? In the distant past, the present or the future? This decision can affect the whole atmosphere and appeal of a film.

For example, film adaptations of Shakespeare plays have sometimes used very modern settings to appeal to a younger audience (like Baz Luhrmann's *Romeo and Juliet*, released in 1997). The stills opposite come from film versions of Jane Austen's novel *Emma* (published in 1816), the story of a rich young woman's attempts to find husbands for her friends. The 1996 version, *Emma*, starring Gwyneth Paltrow, uses a traditional setting while the 1995 version, entitled *Clueless*, is updated and set in an American high school.

Props and set design

Props (short for 'properties') include everything from vehicles to small objects and furnishings. Not only do props tell the audience when the film is set, they can also signal things about the characters. The quality and style of a character's belongings can indicate their status. If a character's house is furnished in an untidy, shoddy style, this could tell the audience that the character is disorganized and/or not very wealthy.

Emma

Clueless

Look at these two film stills.

1 Write down details of the difference in settings which have been used.

2 Describe the props which have been used in each scene. How do they fit with the setting? How do they suit the story?

3 Which film would you most like to see? Why?

4 Make a list of six films – include films set in the past, present and future. For each film, write down some details about the settings and some of the props used.

Casting

Which actors should play the characters? Casting the right person to play a character is very important.

Various well-known actors and actresses have established a reputation for playing certain types of characters. Jim Carrey and Whoopi Goldberg often play comedy roles. Leonardo DiCaprio and Gwyneth Paltrow tend to be cast as romantic leads. How would an audience react if DiCaprio was cast as a villain?

▽

Copy out this grid. Try to think of one male and one female actor who specialize in each character type. Put their names in the second column. In the third, name a film in which each actor plays this kind of role.

Character type	Name of actor/actress	Names of films
Good guy/heroine		
Villain		
Romantic lead		
Comic character		

Clothing, hair and make-up

How should characters be dressed and made up to show the audience something about them? Dark and light clothing colours are often used to signal who are the bad and the good guys. Strong or weak colours can be used to signal something about a character's personality: strong, bright colours often suggest an outgoing, loud or eccentric character, while pastel shades might make a character seem quieter and appear more conventional. Tailored clothes can suggest a character is rich or powerful, whereas an unshaven, untidy appearance can signal a character is down on his luck and poorly off.

*For a Few
Dollars More*

Star Wars: The Phantom Menace

1 Look at these stills.

a Which film genres are these pictures from?

b What information do you get about the characters from their clothing, hair-style and make-up? Can you say which signs tell you what about each character?

2 Discuss and make notes of three films you have seen in which clothing, hair and make-up have been used to influence the audience's feelings about characters. Remember to think about colours of clothing as well as styles.

Positioning, gesture, facial expressions

An important way of signalling meanings to the audience is the way a scene is composed. Which characters will be in the foreground, the background and the centre of the shot? Deciding who is the main focus of a shot affects which character the audience pays most attention to.

The actors' facial expressions, gestures, and body language all have a powerful effect too. Look back at unit 2, pages 22–24 for some hints on what to look for in gestures ('figure signs').

Romeo and Juliet

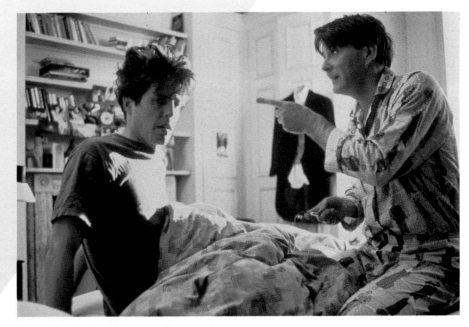

Four Weddings and a Funeral

▽

Study the stills above, then answer the questions.

a Look at the positions of the characters. In each of these shots, which character(s) are we meant to focus on?

b Now look at the characters' gestures. What do the characters' gestures and facial expressions tell us about their feelings towards each other?

Mise-en-scène practice

▽

3

1 Look again at the film stills on pages 99–102. Look at the choice of setting, the props, the clothing, the use of colour. Look at the positioning of the characters, their body gestures and facial gestures.

Now choose one still to study. Use a grid like the one below to organize your thoughts.

a First list in the left-hand column what you can see in the still (denotation). Use the checklist above to remind you what to look for.

b For each item in your list, make notes in the right-hand column on how the film-maker is trying to create meanings by using these various aspects of mise-en-scène (connotation).

This example is based on the picture of Darth Maul.

Denotation	Connotation
(Props, setting) Factory-like setting; light-sabre	Science fiction/futuristic
(Clothing) Black clothes, black shiny gloves	Mysterious, possibly dangerous character
(Make-up, hair) Red and black make-up, red eyes, no hair, horns coming out of skull	Dangerous, threatening character: a bad guy
(Gesture) Light-sabre raised at an angle	Dominant, aggressive, in action

2 Read the following scene outline.

> Officer Gatley opens the door. It is a small room with a window with blinds facing the street. Against one wall is a single bed, a small bedside table and a lamp. Against the other a desk with various objects connected with the occupant's work, and a chair. Framed pictures hang on the wall and some clothes are hanging on a clothes hook. A weapon is lying on the bed.

Imagine you are directing this scene and must decide about all aspects of mise-en-scène (use the checklist at the top of the page).

a Firstly design it as if for a historical drama set in the time of Sherlock Holmes (1880s).

b Secondly design it as if for a futuristic film.

On two sheets of A4 paper, either sketch the interiors of each set with notes indicating style and colour of props and costume – or describe in words how you would construct each version of the scene.

Lighting

When you watch a film you probably never think about the way the scenes are lit. But a director can affect the mood of a scene by using various lighting styles. For example, lighting might be bright, making eyes sparkle and creating a pleasant mood. Or it might be dimmed to create shadows, for a more spooky, sinister mood. Even scenes shot outside may have extra lighting added to create the right atmosphere.

Different colours of lighting can be used to affect the mood: blue and red are often creepy, for example. This can be done using coloured lights or by the way the film is treated after shooting.

The angle of the lighting can also be altered for effect.

Underlighting is when the main lighting comes from below or from the side. This is used in horror films to create shadows and distort appearances.

Toplighting is when the main lighting comes from above – this brightens the look of things and gives a pleasant atmosphere.

Backlighting is when the main lighting comes from behind the subject – this can create silhouettes and a mysterious mood.

Pretty Woman

1 Look at the film stills on these two pages.

  a Which of them use bright lighting and which use dimmed lighting?

  b Which of the stills uses underlighting, backlighting, toplighting?

  c Which of these words would you use to describe the mood and atmosphere of the scenes? *strange, happy, sinister, spooky, pleasant, weird, threatening, gloomy*

2 Face a mirror or a partner, and use a flashlight or lamp to experiment with lighting angles. See what effects you can create by using toplighting, underlighting, and backlighting. If possible get a partner to video or photograph these different lighting effects.

3 Look through magazines, video rental leaflets, newspapers, and posters and put together a presentation showing examples of different uses of lighting to create different moods and atmospheres and to illustrate different film genres.

Scream

ET: The Extra-terrestrial

Camera shots

When you're using a camera, there are a range of possibilities for framing the shot, varying viewpoint and changing what the audience focuses on.

There are two aspects:
the kind of shot –
viewpoint/framing
the way the camera moves.

Here are the main camera shots a film-maker might use:

Long shot (LS) helps to establish where a scene is happening.

Medium shot (MS) shows most of a character's body and some background. Used to show the actions in a straightforward way.

Close-up (CU) helps to involve the audience closely in a scene by focusing on particular objects or faces.

Big close-up (BCU) used to show high emotion and create tension.

High-angle shot views people and objects from above – can make people look small and vulnerable.

Low-angle shot views people and objects from below – can make the audience feel vulnerable.

Point of view shot (POV) shows us what a character is seeing. Helps us to identify with the character, or to create tension, by showing an unknown observer's point of view.

Here are the ways a film-maker can move the camera shot:

Tracking/Dolly shot a camera on wheels moves with the action.

Steadicam shot a hand-held camera follows the action. Can give a jerky feel to a scene, which makes the audience feel they are there.

Zoom shot the camera lens zooms towards or away from the subject. If done quickly, this can be dramatic. If done slowly, it can give a more dreamy mood.

Crane shot a camera on a crane looks down on the action. Or the shot can move dramatically from ground level up to a bird's-eye view.

Pan shot the camera pivots to follow the action.

Constructing a picture sequence

When shooting a scene for a film, a film director must carefully think out the sequence of camera shots. The choice of shots and the way they are edited together both help to create the mood and atmosphere of the film.

For complicated scenes, a film-maker might **storyboard** the scene. A storyboard is a sequence of sketches showing details of camera shots and camera movement. Sometimes an outline of the soundtrack to be used will also be included in the storyboard.

Here is a storyboard for a car-chase scene.

1 Study the storyboard (the first shots have been labelled for you.) Write down what types of shots are used for the rest of the sequence.

2 Look at the range of camera shots used in this sequence.

   a The storyboard moves straight from the high-angle first shot to the low-angle close-up second shot. What effect do you think this sudden change might have on an audience?

   b Look at the last shot of this sequence. Why do you think the film-maker chose a shot from below rather than from above the falling car?

   c Comment on any other ways camera shots have been used here to create suspense and tension.

1 High-angle LS

2 Low-angle CU

3 MS

4 POV shot

5 LS

6

7

8

9

10

Editing

It is in the editing room that a film is really made. Each scene may have been shot using several cameras all shooting at the same time from different angles and positions. Once all the shooting is complete, the director edits the shots. This means cutting the film and assembling it using a variety of shots to create the final film sequence.

The mood and atmosphere of a film are strongly affected by the editing. If a scene is meant to be exciting, then a sequence of very short shots might be edited together. If a mood of calm and quietness is needed, shots that last longer will be edited together.

Changing from shot to shot

The mood of a sequence is also affected by the film-maker's choice of how to change from one shot to the next. Here are some of the main options:

- a **straight cut**: one shot cuts to the next in what feels like a normal sequence.

- a **dissolve/mix shot**: one shot dissolves into the next. This creates a calm, more dreamy mood.

- a **fade-out**: this is when a shot fades to black. This can be used to suggest time passing.

▽

You are going to watch a film sequence.

1 Watch the sequence several times with the sound off. Count each time a shot changes and say out loud what type of shot is being used. When you count, think about the approximate length of each shot and the pace of the editing.

Then answer the following questions:

Denotation (noting what is there)
a How would you describe the pace of the sequence? Is it fast, moderate or slow?

b What kinds of shot changes are used?

Connotation (meanings and effects)
c How does the editing affect the atmosphere and mood of the sequence? Is the mood calm, relaxing and leisurely or exciting and dramatic?

2 Now look more closely at three places where very different camera shots have been used.

Denotation (noting what is there)
a Note what kind of shots have been used.

Connotation (meanings and effects)
b Why do you think the director has chosen to use these particular shots? How is the choice of camera shots meant to affect your feelings about the characters and the actions taking place in the scene? Do you think it works?

The soundtrack

When we watch a film, the key area which perhaps we notice the least but affects us the most is the soundtrack. The soundtrack includes all the sounds which accompany the visual images of a film – music, speaking voices, and sound effects (SFX). (Look back at unit 5 for more detailed information about soundtracks and how they can be made up.)

Opening credits sequence

When you see a new film, you get your first impressions of it during the opening sequence when the written credits are being shown. The credits tell you such things as the name of the film company, the producer, director, maybe the main actors – but not much about the film in terms of its genre or mood. Here, the soundtrack will be one of the main ways of putting across the mood and genre of the film.

Music

This is very powerful in signalling to the audience the emotions they are meant to feel. A fairly ordinary-looking scene can be made to feel very sinister and threatening by using appropriate music – in *Jaws* a pleasant beach scene is made to feel threatening by adding the double-bass music which signals the arrival of the shark.

Sound effects (SFX)

Sound effects such as slamming doors, tyres screeching, and wind whistling are used to heighten the atmosphere of a scene. For example an ordinary-looking night-time scene can be made tense by adding the SFX of a wolf howling.

Voices

These give us strong signals about what a character is like. Sometimes a particular accent or tone of voice will be used by an actor to signal impressions about a character. (See unit 5, pages 78–80 for more about tone of voice and accents.)

Voice-over

If a character's inner thoughts need to be signalled, then a voice-over can be used. This acts like a separate voice being spoken into the ears of the audience. It appears detached from the actions of the characters on screen. It can be used to give background information about a scene, or it can express the more personal thoughts and feelings of a particular character.

Checklist of film signs

Mise-en-scène
    Setting
    Props, set design
    Casting
    Clothing, hair, make-up
    Positioning, gesture, facial expressions
Lighting
Camera shots
Editing
Soundtrack

Checklist of sound signs

SFX
Silence
Speaking voices
    Accent, dialect
    Word sounds
Music
    Instrument sounds

Volume
Pitch
Pace
Rhythm
Tone

▽

1 Suggest sound effects which you would use for the following settings/atmospheres:
  a jungle
  b graveyard
  c pleasant summer's day
  d storm brewing.

2 Suggest the instrument sounds you would get a composer to use to suggest the following mood/atmosphere:
  a magical fantasy
  b mystery/horror
  c tropical paradise.

3 Study the opening title and credits sequence of a film, listening carefully to the soundtrack.
  a Name the instrument sounds used.
  b What kind of rhythm, volume and pace are used?
  c Now explain how the soundtrack is used to suggest the mood and genre of the film.

4 Now watch a few moments of the film itself.
  a Describe how sound signs are used in the film's opening. Do they contrast with the mood of the credits sequence or are they similar?
  b Explain what mood and atmosphere are created in the opening scene by the soundtrack.

Task zone

In this section, you have a chance to put into practice the knowledge you have gained about the way films are constructed. We shall deconstruct some chosen aspects of particular films.

As with all study of media texts the focus for our investigation is the same. We're looking for the way signs are being used. We'll use questions for two-step reading (denotation/connotation) and the TAPE key questions.

We shall be looking mainly at feature films which tell a story. So we need to look at the way film signs are used for the narrative purpose – that is, to tell the audience about the characters and the story-line.

Deconstruction case study 1:

A Close Shave (Wallace and Gromit): Aardman Animations 1995

This is a film created using animation. Although the production techniques of animation are very different from normal film-making, the use of film language is much the same.

We have selected a few short sequences from the film to study in detail. You could examine one or all of the scenes. The questions on two scenes are here. Your teacher may also give you general questions and questions on a third sequence.

First, view the whole film (about 30 minutes) and discuss what you have seen. Then look in more detail at one or more of the individual sequences.

> **TAPE**
>
> **T**ype
> What type of text is this? What codes does it use?
>
> **A**udience
> Who is it aimed at? Age? Gender? Interests?
>
> **P**urpose
> What is this text trying to do? What is it trying to make its audience think and feel, in order to do this?
>
> **E**ffectiveness
> Do you think the text would achieve its purpose?

9

10

Sequence 1 (Opening scene: the truck and the escape of Shaun the sheep)

Watch from the beginning up to where the title appears.

1 **Props, setting:** look first at the way Wallace's bedroom is furnished.

   a List the props that you see.

   b What impression of Wallace's personality do the props give us?

2 **Camera shots:**

   a What kind of shot is used right at the start of the film? How does the camera move?

   b The opening shot ends with a close-up of a knife which falls and sticks in the floor. Why do you think the knife has been used in this way?

3 **Soundtrack:** when the knife falls the title appears.

   a How does the soundtrack change at this point? What instrument sounds go with the title?

   b What mood is created when the title appears?

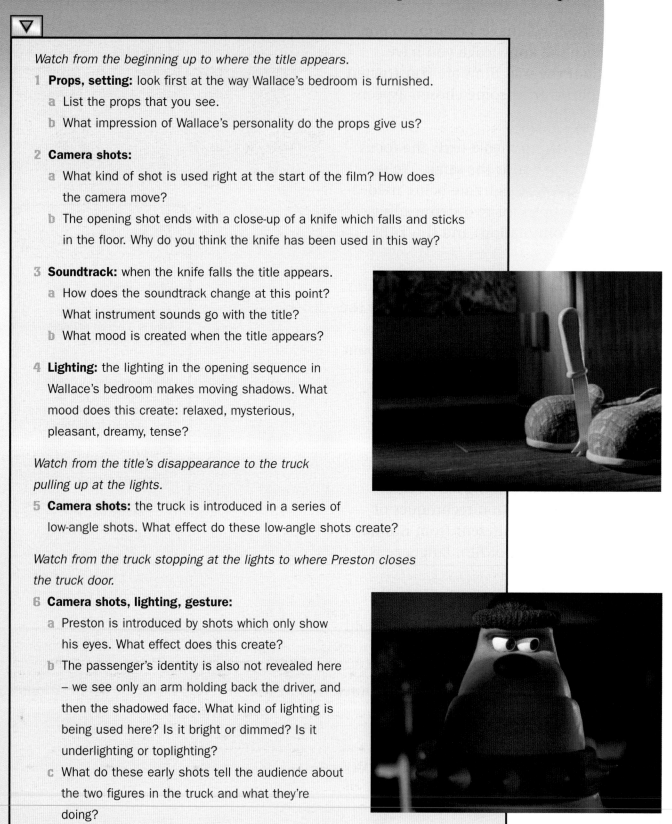

4 **Lighting:** the lighting in the opening sequence in Wallace's bedroom makes moving shadows. What mood does this create: relaxed, mysterious, pleasant, dreamy, tense?

Watch from the title's disappearance to the truck pulling up at the lights.

5 **Camera shots:** the truck is introduced in a series of low-angle shots. What effect do these low-angle shots create?

Watch from the truck stopping at the lights to where Preston closes the truck door.

6 **Camera shots, lighting, gesture:**

   a Preston is introduced by shots which only show his eyes. What effect does this create?

   b The passenger's identity is also not revealed here – we see only an arm holding back the driver, and then the shadowed face. What kind of lighting is being used here? Is it bright or dimmed? Is it underlighting or toplighting?

   c What do these early shots tell the audience about the two figures in the truck and what they're doing?

Watch again from the title's disappearance to where Gromit runs out of wool.

7   Gestures, facial expression, props/setting: throughout this first scene, Gromit is in bed knitting.

   a Describe the way the bedroom is furnished. Look at his facial expression and his reactions to what he hears.

   b What are your first impressions of Gromit's personality, his thoughts and feelings? Explain what has created these impressions for you.

Watch this section again.

8   Soundtrack – SFX and music: sound is extremely important in creating the atmosphere of the opening scene.

   a List seven sound effects which are used in this opening scene.

   b Listen for when music is used. Which instrument sounds do you hear?

   c Why do you think these instrument sounds and SFX were used – what feelings do they create?

Watch from Gromit running out of wool to Wallace landing at the breakfast table.

9   Editing: all the shot changes in the opening scene are straight cuts, except the final shot change.

   a What kind of shot change is used to end the scene and start the breakfast scene?

   b Why was this different shot change used?

10 Lighting:

   a How is the breakfast scene lit differently from the opening scene?

   b How would you describe the atmosphere of the opening scene compared to that of the breakfast scene?

Watch the whole sequence again.

11 Your TAPE summary: how do you rate this sequence? Would you say that the way film signs have been used will have the desired effect on the target audience? Give reasons for your answer.

Sequence 2 (An intruder in the house)

For this scene, you have the help of a storyboard which uses Nick Park's original storyboard sketches. This storyboard has been provided to help you identify the different shots in this sequence, and to see how they are combined with dialogue, SFX and music. Use it as well as the video to help you answer the questions.

shot 1 – 2 secs
Camera notes: CU panning right – into doorway to LS
Soundtrack: SFX: creaking door, footsteps
Music: quiet strings

shot 2 – 2 secs
Camera notes: CU: Gromit
Soundtrack: Music: quiet strings

shot 3 – 1 sec
Camera notes: Slow zoom to CU of hallway
Soundtrack: Silence

shot 4 – 1 sec
Camera notes: CU: Gromit
Soundtrack: W: I think...

shot 5 – 2 secs
Camera notes: MS: Wallace
Soundtrack: W: ... I'll make my own porridge.

shot 6 – 1 sec
Camera notes: CU: Gromit
Soundtrack: SFX: footsteps
Music: strings

shot 7 – 2 secs
Camera notes: LS: Gromit in hallway
Soundtrack: Music: low strings
SFX: footsteps

shot 8 – 6 secs
Camera notes: CU: Gromit and plant
Soundtrack: Music: low strings
SFX: footsteps, chewing sound

shot 9 – 5 secs
Camera notes: CU porridge packet
Soundtrack: SFX: picking object off shelf
W: *Well I'll be...*
SFX: porridge spilling

shot 10 – 3 secs
Camera notes: CU: cheese, Wallace behind
Soundtrack: Music: strings
W: *Have you been peckish during the night?*

shot 11 – 5 secs
Camera notes: CU: Gromit
Soundtrack: Music: strings
W: *... only someone's been at me cheese.*
SFX: footsteps
Moment of silence as Gromit turns

shot 12 – 4 secs
Camera notes: CU: Gromit at plant
Soundtrack: Music: low strings
SFX: footsteps

shot 13 – 1 sec
Camera notes: CU: Gromit
Soundtrack: SFX: twig snapping

shot 14 – 3 secs
Camera notes: MS: leaf falling then fast zoom to CU
Soundtrack: Second of silence then Music: strings

shot 15 – 3 secs
Camera notes: CU: Gromit
Soundtrack: W: *Well I don't know...*
Music: low strings

shot 16 – 3 secs
Camera notes: CU: Gromit then fast refocus to LS on Wallace
Soundtrack: Music: strings
W: *There's something very fishy going on.*

shot 17 – 7 secs
Camera notes: CU: newspaper with Wallace behind
Soundtrack: SFX: newspaper rustling
Music: harp chord
W: *Uh? D'you think we should get the, um, pest control people in?*
SFX: telephone ringing

shot 18 – 5 secs
Camera notes: MS: Shaun and Wallace
Soundtrack: SFX: newspaper rustling, chewing, telephone receiver picked up
W: *Hello, Wallace & Gromit's Wash 'n' Go window cleaning service. May we be of assistance?*

shot 19 – 6 secs
Camera notes: CU: Shaun
Soundtrack: Wend: *Hello, yes. My windows could do with a jolly good clean.*

shot 20 – 2 secs
Camera notes: CU: telephone and speaker
Soundtrack: Wend: *... the wool shop in the high street.*

shot 21 – 3 secs
Camera notes: MS: Gromit pulling lever
Soundtrack: Wend: *Soon as you can.*
SFX: Lever noise
W: *On our way, madam.*

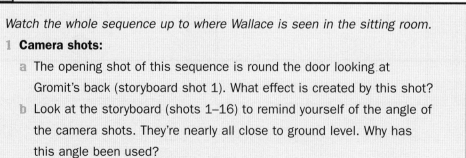

Watch the whole sequence up to where Wallace is seen in the sitting room.

1 **Camera shots:**

  a The opening shot of this sequence is round the door looking at Gromit's back (storyboard shot 1). What effect is created by this shot?

  b Look at the storyboard (shots 1–16) to remind yourself of the angle of the camera shots. They're nearly all close to ground level. Why has this angle been used?

  c Can you spot any POV (point of view) shots in this sequence? Whose points of view are represented?

Watch the same section again.

2 **Soundtrack:** a tense atmosphere is created in this sequence by the soundtrack.

  a Make a list of the SFX which are used.

  b Moments of silence are used with a number of the shots (3, 11, and 14 in the storyboard). What effect does the use of silence have on the atmosphere?

  c What feelings are created by the use of stringed instruments in the music?

Watch again if necessary – just up to where Shaun passes Gromit in the hall.

3 **Soundtrack – speech:** The characters of Wallace and Gromit react differently when they discover something strange is going on. Remind yourself about what Wallace says in shots 4–5. What is he particularly upset about?

Watch the bit with Wallace on the phone.

4 **Setting, props:** Look at the furnishings used in the living room where Wallace is reading the chewed newspaper.

  a List the props that you notice.

  b What do they tell us about Wallace's personality?

5 **Narrative clues:** The central story-line of the film concerns wool shortage and sheep rustling. Where are clues about this story-line given in this scene?

Watch from Wallace speaking on the phone to Wallace going through the ceiling.

6 **Soundtrack – music:**

  a How does the soundtrack change after Wallace has put down the phone? Describe the soundtrack for the next sequence when Wallace prepares for work.

  b What instrument sounds are now used?

  c How is the mood now different from the 'intruder' sequence?

Watch the whole sequence again.

7 **Your TAPE summary:** how do you rate this sequence? Would you say that the way film signs have been used will have the desired effect on the target audience? Give reasons for your answer.

Deconstruction case study 2:

Macbeth (Cromwell Films 1996)

We have selected a few sequences from the film to study in detail. You could examine one or all of the scenes. The questions on two scenes are here. Your teacher may also give you general questions and questions on a third sequence.

First, watch enough of the film to get a clear idea of the characters and the opening events – perhaps about 40 minutes, up to the knocking at the door just after Duncan's murder.

After your initial viewing, discuss what you have seen. Then look in more detail at one or more of the individual sequences.

Sequence 1 (The battle scene up to Macbeth and Banquo's meeting with the witches: Act 1 Scenes 1–3 of the play)

The battle scene

Watch the whole section, then the first half of the battle scene – up to where Macbeth comes striding towards the camera.

1 **Clothing, figure signs, camera shots:**

  a When we see the three witches for the very first time, where are they? What are they doing? How are they dressed?

  b What kind of camera shot is used to present them to the viewer? What first impression do you get of the three witches from this opening shot?

  c The first shot of Macbeth is a medium shot with him moving towards the audience. How does he move? How does he fight? What facial expressions does he show? How is he dressed? What make-up does he have on? What is his hair like? Is he clean-shaven or bearded?

  d Why has the film-maker chosen this as the opening shot of Macbeth? What impressions does it give us of him?

Watch the beginning of the battle again with the sound off.

2 **Camera shots, editing:** The battle is mainly shot in a series of close-ups.

   a How does this use of close-ups affect the audience's impression of the battle?

   b Count out loud every time the shot changes. How would you describe the pace of the editing?

   c What atmosphere does this pace of editing create?

Watch from Macbeth coming towards the camera to when Macbeth kills his victim.

3 **Camera shots:** When Macbeth is about to kill the enemy soldier, low-angle close-up shots looking up at Macbeth are used, with high-angle close-up shots looking down at his enemy. How are these camera angles meant to affect the audience?

4 **Figure signs:** Study Macbeth's expression as he looks down at the enemy soldier and kills him.

   a Is he angry? Does he seem to enjoy what he is doing?

   b What does this tell you about Macbeth's character?

5 **Editing, soundtrack:**

   a When Macbeth is about to kill his enemy, the pace of the editing slows down. Why is this done?

   b How does the soundtrack change at this point from that of the earlier battle shots? How does this affect the mood of the scene at this point?

   c At this point a split second shot of the three witches is inserted into the sequence. Why has this been done?

After the battle

Watch from Macbeth killing his victim to when the witches say 'There to meet with Macbeth'.

6 **Setting, camera shots, figure signs:** After the battle, the witches run down to the beach.

   a What kinds of camera shots are used as they are running? Why have these shots been used?

   b What mood are the witches in as they sit on the beach?

Watch from the end of the witches' scene to where Macbeth and Banquo get off their horses.

7 **Editing, soundtrack:** During the battle, straight cuts are used for shot changes.

   a After the battle, when we see Macbeth and Banquo on horseback, what kind of shot changes are used? How does this change the mood of the film?

   b Describe the sound signs (instrument sounds, pace, etc.) used in the soundtrack here. What mood is created by this use of sound signs?

The meeting with the witches

Watch from where Macbeth and Banquo get off their horses to the end of Banquo's speech.

8 **Camera shots, soundtrack:**

   a What kinds of camera shots are used when the witches first appear and then when each of them speaks?

   b When Banquo starts to speak and walk around the witches a steadicam shot is used. What is the effect of using a steadicam shot here rather than a series of separate camera shots to follow his movements?

   c What kinds of SFX are used during the meeting with the witches? What mood do these SFX create?

Watch from the end of Banquo's speech to when the witches have all vanished.

9 **Facial expressions, gesture, voice:** Which one of the witches most unsettles Macbeth? What causes him to be unsettled?

10 **Lighting, soundtrack:**

   a In what way do the lighting and soundtrack change from when the witches are present to after they have vanished?

   b Why do you think this is done?

Watch the whole sequence again.

11 The purpose of the battle scene and the scene with the witches is to:

   ■ start the film in a powerful and dramatic way

   ■ establish some first impressions of the key characters of Macbeth and Banquo.

To what extent do you think the filming of the scene achieves its purposes?

Sequence 2 (The 'dagger' scene – from Macbeth bidding Banquo goodnight, to the bell which 'summons thee to heaven or to hell': Act 2 Scene 1 of the play)

This storyboard has been provided to help you identify the different shots in the chapel part of the sequence, and see how they are combined with dialogue, SFX and music. Use it as well as the video to help you answer the questions.

shot 1 – 3 secs
Camera notes: BCU: window with twigs out of focus
Soundtrack: Music: slow, deep strings
SFX: twigs tapping on window

shot 2 – 2 secs
Camera notes: BCU: candle
Soundtrack: Music: slow strings
SFX: tapping of twigs on window

shot 3 – 9 secs
Camera notes: MS: Macbeth enters chapel and approaches camera
Soundtrack: Music: strings, slow woodwind tune
SFX: twigs scratching on window

shot 4 – 3 secs
Camera notes: Low-angle CU: cross
Soundtrack: Music: strings
SFX: twigs on window

shot 5 – 9 secs
Camera notes: MS: Macbeth
Soundtrack: Music: strings
SFX: thunder, twigs scratching window

shot 6 – 9 secs
Camera notes: CU of twigs on window tilting down to CU of cross
Soundtrack: Music: strings
SFX: twigs tapping, wind noise

shot 7 – 5 secs
Camera notes: CU: Macbeth, changing
to BCU
Soundtrack: Music: strings

shot 8 – 6 secs
Camera notes: MS: Macbeth kneeling
Soundtrack: Music: strings
SFX: thunder, twigs against window

shot 9 – 3 secs
Camera notes: Low-angle POV CU:
cross as window behind blows open
Soundtrack: Music: strings
SFX: thunder

shot 10 – 1 sec
Camera notes: High-angle CU: Macbeth
looking up
Soundtrack: Music: strings
Macbeth gasps

shot 11 – 2 secs
Camera notes: POV CU: shadow of cross
on floor
Soundtrack: Voice-over (Macbeth): *Is
this a dagger...*
Music: strings

shot 12 – 3 secs
Camera notes: High-angle CU: Macbeth
Soundtrack: VO: ... *which I see before
me,* ...
Music: strings

shot 13 – 7 secs
Camera notes: High-angle BCU of
shadow, tilting up length of arm to CU
of Macbeth's face as he tries to grasp
the 'dagger'
Soundtrack: VO: ...*the handle toward my
hand? Come, let me clutch thee. I have
thee not, and yet...*
Music: strings, woodwind tune

shot 14 – 6 secs
Camera notes: High-angle MS: Macbeth
stooping close to the floor
Soundtrack: VO: ...*I see thee still. Art
thou not, fatal vision, sensible to feeling
as to...*
Music: strings, woodwind

shot 15 – 10 secs
Camera notes: CU: Macbeth
Soundtrack: VO: ... *sight? or art thou
but a dagger of the mind, a false
creation, proceeding from the heat-
oppressed brain? I see thee yet, in form
as palpable as this which now I draw.*
Music: strings
SFX: wind

shot 16 – 5 secs
Camera notes: High-angle MS: Macbeth
Soundtrack: VO: *Thou marshall'st me the way that I was going; and such an instrument I was to use.*
Music: strings SFX: wind

shot 17 – 7 secs
Camera notes: CU: Macbeth
Soundtrack: VO: *Mine eyes are made the fools o' th' other senses, or else worth all the rest. I see thee still;*
Music: strings SFX: wind

shot 18 – 13 secs
Camera notes: High-angle MS: Macbeth kneeling, then he gets up
Soundtrack: VO: *And on thy blade [...] Now o'er the one...*
SFX: wind

shot 19 – 2 secs
Camera notes: Low-angle CU: cross
Soundtrack: VO: *... half-world, nature...*
Music: strings, pipes
SFX: wind

shot 20 – 40 secs
Camera notes: Slow panning CU following Macbeth moving right to left
Soundtrack: VO: *... seems dead, and [...] Words to the heat of deeds too cold breath gives.*
Music: strings, pipes SFX: wind

shot 21 – 4 secs
Camera notes: MS: Macbeth and dagger
Soundtrack: Music: strings
SFX: wind moaning

shot 22 – 3 secs
Camera notes: Low-angle MS: Lady Macbeth tolls the bell (underlit)
Soundtrack: Music: harp
SFX: wind, bell

shot 23 – 18 secs
Camera notes: CU: Macbeth
Soundtrack: Macbeth: *I go, and it is done; the bell invites me. Hear it not, Duncan, for it is a knell that summons thee to heaven or to hell.*
Music: harp, choir voices
SFX: bell, wind, thunder

▽

Watch the whole sequence, then from the beginning to where Macbeth goes back into the castle from the battlements.

1 **Lighting:** The opening sequence with Banquo and Macbeth is underlit with a blue light. What mood is created by this style of lighting?

2 **Soundtrack:** What SFX are used when Banquo leaves Macbeth on his own? How do they affect the atmosphere?

Watch from where Macbeth enters the chapel to where he stands up, ready to leave.

3 **Adaptation – setting, props:** In the play, Macbeth sees the dagger in a courtyard, not a chapel. Why do you think the film-maker set this scene in a chapel, using a cross to form the dagger?

4 **Camera shots, positioning:**

a Look at shots 1–9 in the storyboard, ending with a low-angle POV shot of the cross from Macbeth's point of view. What effect is this POV shot intended to have on the audience?

b This scene includes twigs rattling on a moonlit window, a flickering candle flame, a window opened by a strange rush of wind. From which film genre have these techniques been borrowed? Why have they been used in this scene?

Watch this section again.

5 **Soundtrack:** What SFX are used during the chapel scene? What effect are these SFX intended to have on the atmosphere of the scene?

Watch from where Macbeth stands up to 'that summons thee to heaven or to hell'.

6 **Lighting:** Towards the end of the chapel scene, there is a brief shot of Lady Macbeth tolling the bell.

a What sort of lighting is used for this shot?

b What impression does this give of Lady Macbeth?

Watch the whole sequence again.

7 The purpose of the 'dagger' scene is to:

■ take us into the troubled mind of Macbeth

■ build up the suspense and tension before the murder scene.

To what extent do you think the filming of the scene achieves its purposes?

Construction task: film adaptation

Books are often adapted into films. These activities are based on an extract from *The Cybil War* by Betsy Byars. You will have a go at turning the extract into a screenplay, planning the aspects of mise-en-scène, and creating a storyboard.

Checklist of film signs

Mise-en-scène
  Setting
  Props, set design
  Casting
  Clothing, hair, make-up
  Positioning, gesture, facial expressions
Lighting
Camera shots
Editing
Soundtrack

1 Writing a screenplay

Start by trying to picture the scene in your mind. Think about what you want your audience to see and hear. (In the book, the setting is American – but you don't have to keep to that if you want to change it.)

4
6
8

Remember to include details of setting, characters' actions and words, information about the soundtrack, indicating SFX and type of music, and initial ideas for camera shots and lighting. Don't worry: you can add more detail later, as you tackle the other parts of the task.

In this scene Tony Angotti and his friend Simon have planned to meet two girls at the cinema. Simon's not very keen to go and things are already going wrong.

TAPE

Type
What type of text am I constructing? What codes can I use?

Audience
Who is it aimed at? Age? Gender? Interests?

Purpose
What is it trying to do? How shall I try to do this? (How do I want the audience to feel? How can I use signs to get this response?)

Effectiveness
Will it work? (Show a friend, check it out and change bits if necessary.)

Suddenly Tony Angotti burst through the Mall doors. He ran across the parking lot, dodging cars like he was on the football field.

'Disaster,' he gasped when he got to Simon. The force of his movement caused them to swing round like children on the playground.

'What happened?' Simon asked. His voice rose with sudden hope. 'Harriet didn't come?'

'Worse! They're waiting *outside* the movie theatre.' He grabbed Simon's shoulders and shook him to get the meaning to go down. 'I told them *inside*, you know, so we don't have to pay!'

'Well –'

'And now they're *outside*!' His eyes shifted to Simon's pocket. 'How much money have you got?'

'Three dollars.'

'Well it's two dollars to get in, and that's what I've got – two dollars! And even for that I have to stoop down and pretend I'm a child!'

2 Planning

13 Now that you have your screenplay you need to plan the shooting of the scene. Your teacher can give you a 'Scene detail sheet' to help you plan how you will construct the scene.

a **Setting:** where will you place the two actors for the shooting of this scene? What will be in the background? Will it take place during the day or at night? What will the weather be like?

b **Casting, clothing, make-up:** how will you cast the parts of the characters? Think about their age and physical appearance. Once you have thought who will act the parts, decide on the characters' clothing and hair-styles.

c **Lighting:** how will the shots be lit? For example, will the boys be talking in a dark side alley or in a sunny street? If it's set at night how will you light their faces – will you use toplighting, underlighting or backlighting? Will the lighting be bright or dim?

d **Camera shots:** in your screenplay you should have started indicating the types of camera shots to be used. Look back as you work through it and add more notes if you are getting further ideas from thinking more about the other aspects.

Write some notes to say why you have decided to do things as you have.

3 Storyboarding your screenplay

 Now use a 'Storyboard sheet' to storyboard the scene. The storyboard should show sketches of the sequence of shots, notes on camera movement, and details of the soundtrack which accompanies the shots.

a As you sketch your storyboard, think carefully about each shot, and try to show in more detail what will be shown on the screen for each shot.

b **Camera shots:** give camera notes for each shot, to indicate details of camera movement and what is shown.

c **Editing:** indicate on your storyboard how long each shot should last, to give an idea of the pace. (You could also include the type of shot change – cut, mix or fade.)

d **Soundtrack:** include notes about the sounds which will accompany the visuals. Apart from the boys' voices will there be SFX and music, maybe a voice-over? Make notes on the type of music, giving details of instrument sounds, pace, rhythm, volume, pitch and tone.

Write some notes to say why you have decided to do things as you have.

Glossary

accent the way words and sentences are pronounced, depending on the region or country the speaker comes from.

adjective tag a descriptive word or phrase attached to a noun, e.g. _Father-of-four_ Tom Long.

alliteration using words close together which contain the same consonant sound.

assonance using words close together which begin with the same vowel sound.

backlighting lighting which comes from behind the subject.

camera shot a technical term for what is shown on screen in a film: this involves distance e.g. _long shot_ and viewpoint e.g. _low angle shot._

composition the process of putting signs together to make a text.

dialect the form of words and grammar used in speech.

editing the process of choosing and putting together the shots that make up a film sequence.

emotive language choosing words to affect the reader's feelings.

figure signs hand and facial gestures, body language, clothing, etc.

genre a type or category of film or book.

high-level viewpoint when the reader views an image from above eye level.

imagery the use of language to create a powerful picture in the reader's mind. (See _simile_, _metaphor_ and _personification_.)

imperative the verb form which tells the reader to do something, e.g. _Get up!_

interrogative the verb form which asks the reader a question, e.g. _Looking for a bargain?_

location the place where a scene is supposed to be happening.

low-level viewpoint when the reader views an image from below eye level.

metaphor imagery where something is described as something else e.g. _He was a tornado in midfield._

mise-en-scène what is put into a film scene: includes casting, location, props, clothing, make-up, actors' positioning and gestures.

pace speed (of speech, music, or shot changes).

personification imagery where something is given human qualities, e.g. _The wind screamed._

pitch how high or low a sound is.

presentational devices techniques used in printed texts to attract the reader's attention, e.g. headlines, bullet points, underlining.

proportion whether representations of people or objects are a realistic size and shape or whether they are _out of proportion_ as in, say, cartoons or horror films.

props short for 'properties' – objects, furnishings, etc. in visual media.

rhetorical question a question which is asked for effect, e.g. _Do you lack confidence?_

setting the place and time where a film scene is supposed to be happening.

SFX sound effects: sounds added to a radio or film recording to create a mood or suggest a location.

simile imagery which compares one thing to another, using the words _like_ or _as_, e.g. _Her hair was like silk._

soundtrack sounds which accompany a moving image text, including voices, music, SFX.

syntax the way words are put together in sentences, including the order of the words and the length of sentences.

texture the way the surface of things looks, e.g. rough, smooth, silky, coarse.

tone the feeling created by hearing a sound, e.g. gentle, aggressive.

toplighting lighting which comes from above the subject.

underlighting lighting which comes from below or to the side of the subject.

viewpoint the position from which the audience views an image: from high up or low down, close-up or far away.

Acknowledgments

The Publisher would like to thank the following for permission to reproduce photographs:

Aardman Animations/Wallace & Gromit Ltd: pp 112, 113, 114, 115, 116, 117; BBC News: p 15; AFP: p 71 (right); Collections/Paul Bryans: p 8 (left); Collections/Nigel French: p 8 (right); Corbis UK Ltd/Kit Houghton: p 49; Corbis UK Ltd/David Tumley: p 20; Corel Professional Photos: pp 19 (bottom left), 21, 28, 29 (bottom), 85 (bottom); Cromwell Productions: pp 118, 119, 120, 124; Egmont Fleetway Ltd: p 35; Express Newspapers: p 25 (bottom); Getty One/Stone: pp 29 (top), 70 (left); The Ronald Grant Archive/Twentieth Century Fox: p 11; The Ronald Grant Archive/Lucas Film: p 14; The Ronald Grant Archive: p 24; Media Insurance Services/AXA/Ridley Media: p 37; The Moviestore Collection: pp 19 (top right), 99 (top), 101 (both), 102 (bottom), 104, 105 (both); National News/Jeff Moore: p 71 (left); Paramount (Courtesy Kobal): p 102 (top); Photodisc: pp 51, 73, 84, 85; Pictorial Press: p 99 (bottom); Popperfoto: pp 18, 30 (bottom), 70 (right); Rex Features: p 31; Superstock: p 24; Sygma: p 30 (top & middle).

Artwork is by Lee Sullivan: pp 106, 107, 121, 122, 123.

Other photographs and artwork: Oxford University Press.

We are grateful to the following for permission to reprint copyright material:

British Heart Foundation for 'Look After Your Heart', extract from *Body File* newsletter, copyright © British Heart Foundation 1998. **Buena Vista Home Entertainment Ltd** for cover of *Global Video* instore magazine, July 1999, copyright © Buena Vista Home Entertainment 1999. **Dark Horse Comics** for extracts from *Buffy the Vampire Slayer* graphic novel, Buffy the Vampire Slayer™ and © copyright 2001, Twentieth Century Fox Film Corporation. All rights reserved. TM designates a trademark of Twentieth Century Fox Film Corporation. Dark Horse Comics® and the Dark Horse logo are trademarks of Dark Horse Comics, Inc., registered in various categories and countries. All rights reserved. **Future Publishing Ltd** for front cover and extracts from reviews, *PlayStation Max Magazine*, Issue 3, March 1999.

Guardian Newspapers Ltd for articles, 'Mother Saves Her Baby's Life', *The Guardian*, 8.4.99 and 'Teachers Defiant on Holiday Cuts' by Rebecca Smithers, *The Guardian*, 8.4.99, both copyright © The Guardian 1999; and extracts from article, 'Mystery of a Quiet Man' by Owen Bowcott and Jon Henley, *The Guardian*, 7.9.97, copyright © The Guardian 1997. **ISL Marketing AG** for back covers of *FIFA World Cup Guide for Kids* (Carlton Books, 1998) and *FIFA World Cup Superstars* (Carlton Books, 1998). All rights reserved. **Cameron Mackintosh Ltd** for 'Exclusive seat offer' advertisement from Radio Times, designed by Dewynters plc, London, and TM©. All rights reserved. **Mirror Syndication International** for extracts from articles, 'Speed Freak' by Peter Allen and Ted Oliver, *The Mirror*, 3.9.97, 'Why Nato's Canny Cockney Kid is now Worth Megadosh' by Jane Kerr, *The Mirror*, 8.4.99, 'Raging Gun Battle Traps Blitzed Brits' by Graham Brough, *The Mirror*, 16.10.97, and 'Tot Saved by Mum' by Maxine Frith, *The Mirror*, 8.4.99. **National Society for the Prevention of Cruelty to Children** for extract from leaflet 'Handle with Care' (NSPCC, 1995). **News International Syndication** for articles, 'Fame bid by Gum', *The Sun*, London, 12.10.97 and 'A Token of our Esteem for Jo' by Tim Spanton, *The Sun*, London, 9.4.99; and for articles, 'Imogen's a Bubbly Bike Babe' by Sean O'Brien, *The News of the World*, 19.10.97, extract from article, 'JFK's Son Killed in Plane Crash' by David Jeffs, *The News of the World*, 18.7.99; and for video cassette cover for *Monica Grenfell's Get Back Into Your Jeans Workout*; all copyright © News International Newspapers Ltd. **The Random House Group Ltd** for extract from *The Cybil War* by Betsy Byars (Bodley Head, 1981). **Mrs Anne Serraillier** for extract from *The Silver Sword* by Ian Serraillier (Jonathan Cape, 1956).

We would also like to thank the following for permission to use publicity materials:

Carlisle City Council for *Places to Visit 1999* leaflet cover; **Chessington World of Adventures** for leaflet cover; **Southern Tourist Board** for *Best of Dorset* leaflet cover; **THE Games Ltd** for *Zelda* advertisement; **Unique Vacations (UK) Ltd** for Sandals 'Feel the Magic of the Caribbean' advertisement; **The York Dungeon** for website.